For Diana, our Artemis,

Dream Stories
Recovering the Inner Mystic

With Love,

Connie Calders Kellie M

Book cover design by Todd Engel

Book cover original art by Kellie Meisl.

Printed in the United States of America.

Booklocker.com, Inc.
2009

Portions of the following chapters were previously published in *Dream Network Journal* (www.dreamnetwork.net):

Chapter 1 Shamanic Dreamtime
Chapter 4 Casting the Heroine
Chapter 5 Waking Dream
Chapter 6 Planes, Dreams and Eagle Feathers
Chapter 9 Dream Themes

Dream Stories
Recovering the Inner Mystic

Connie Caldes and Kellie Meisl

Dedication

Connie and Kellie dedicate this book to their children, Benjamin, David and Tara, for providing the inspiration to live more creative lives.

Acknowledgements By Connie

I am deeply grateful to Kellie Meisl for her love and friendship for the past 21 years and for working tirelessly to help resolve life's issues, co-teach workshops, create art and participate in the creation of this book.

I extend my gratitude to Sandra Ingerman for all of the teaching she has provided me in the last decade. Her constant reminder to strip away ego has shaped my life and my work.

Thank you to Richard Kluth, Claudia Ricci, Sandra Ingerman, Stanley Krippner and Roberta Ossana for their wonderful support in publishing this book.

Many heartfelt thanks to my fellow cancer survivors, Laurie Mick, Kathy Hart, Linda Ruberto, Claudia Ricci and Maureen Forestell for all of their love in recovering from breast cancer. I am also deeply grateful to Bernie Siegel for his Exceptional Cancer Patient on-line forum.

I am forever thankful to Sue Langman, Deborah Nedde, Vicki Shulof and Tom Tanner for their endless support, wisdom and unwavering friendship, and to Vicki Woodyard for being my *I've Never Met Her in Person* spiritual pal.

I would also like to thank my children, Tara and David Mah, and brother, George Caldes for their wonderful spirits and my parents, Justine Caldes and Theodore G. Caldes for bringing me into this world.

And, finally, I would like to thank my helping spirits, including my Greek grandparents Papou and Chrisoula, for guiding me in healing, teaching and finding the *inner mystic*.

Acknowledgements By Kellie

My heartfelt thanks to my long time friend, Connie Caldes for your openness with sharing dreams, your willingness to sift through mountains of life issues with me, and for your availability to me on a moment's notice, even if that means meeting for tea in our pajamas! Working on this project with you has taught me invaluable life lessons.

I am grateful to my husband Steve Meisl for gifting me with my first computer so I could "write my book". You supported me through this project, the endless hours of learning, creating, writing, teaching, and compromised schedules it took. Thank you to my son Benjamin Meisl for his inspiration and attention to my project. Your big-hearted interest was no small feat at the age of eleven.

I am thankful to my family, especially my parents, Andrea and Richard Powers, for listening to my dreams and encouraging me to become an artist; my sister and brother, Colleen Powers and Richard Powers, for their love and constant guidance; and my soul sisters, Marcia Mentrup and Lisa Powers for cheering me on each step of the way; and my godmother, Aunt Rosemary, whose support I still receive in dreams.

Gratitude to my soul friend, Cathy Salvini, for sharing dreams daily and never missing an important detail. Appreciation to Lori Palma and Amy Cassotta.

Thanks to Richard Kluth, Claudia Ricci, Sandra Ingerman, Stanley Krippner and Roberta Ossana for their help with this book.

And appreciation to the helping spirits of my dreams who remind me how to be happy and whole.

A collection of personal stories shared between two women, which span a decade and weave friendship, cycles of birth and death, breast cancer, inter-generational healing, instruction, teaching and recovery together through dreams, art, shamanic practice and imaginative writing.

Table of Contents

About the Authors

CONNIE CALDES

Connie Caldes enjoys the study of shamanism, dreams, human consciousness and energy medicine. She has trained with Sandra Ingerman, *The Foundation for Shamanic Studies*, *The Monroe Institute*, Stanley Krippner, *The New England Dreamwork Institute*, Malidoma Somé, Sobonfu Somé and Judith Orloff. She has completed the *Foundation for Shamanic Studies Three Year Program* and *Sandra Ingerman's Two Year Shamanic Teacher Training* and is listed as a shamanic practitioner and teacher on www.shamanicteachers.com. Connie holds a Bachelor of Science in Chemical Engineering from *Tufts University*. As a breast cancer survivor, she works diligently to raise awareness about breast cancer and healing after illness. Her writing has been published in *Dream Network Journal*. She is a shamanic practitioner and a Reiki master and teaches shamanism and dreamwork regularly. Connie lives with her two children in the Berkshire Mountains of Massachusetts and can be reached at ShamanicDreamtime@gmail.com or through her website, www.ShamanicDreamtime.com.

KELLIE MEISL

Kellie Meisl holds a Bachelor of Science degree in Education from *North Adams State College*. She completed a two-year program in advanced shamanism receiving her training with Sandra Ingerman, *The Foundation for Shamanic Studies* and Connie Caldes. She studied energy healing with Joyce Morris and *The Monroe Institute*. An artist, she uses her dreams as a springboard for her artwork. For the past decade, she has created art annually for community causes including the *Pittsfield Garden Tour* and the *Think Pink Breast Cancer Awareness Art Exhibit*. In 2008, she designed the *Hope Mandala*, co-created with Tibetan monks and *The Breast Health Team* at Pittsfield's Colonial Theater. She teaches *DreamArt* classes privately and in her community at the Lichtenstein Center for the Arts. Kellie is an active volunteer for the local public school system where she was a teacher until the birth of her son. Her writing has been published in *Dream Network Journal*. She lives in the Berkshires with her husband and son and can be reached at kellie.meisl@gmail.com or through her website at www.KellieMeislDreamArt.com.

Preface

Over twenty years ago, Connie and Kellie met in a twelve-step program based on Robin Norwood's book, *Women Who Love Too Much*. Their friendship was founded on the idea of healing relationships and grew over the years as marriages were formed and children were born. Each woman had her own triumphs and struggles including experiences with shifting from traditional employment to the role of mother, loss of relationships, death of family members and breast cancer. Connie and Kellie stood by each other through all of these initiations that life offered. And, most importantly, they spoke daily of their common desire to find hope and meaning in their lives. While the two were home with very young sons, their discussions on living life through the twelve steps opened into deeper territory. They started to talk about their sleeping dreams and the healing ideas that sprang from them. They further discussed many avenues of alternative healing. Connie and Kellie read book after book and attended workshop after workshop, questing for a new spiritual vision of life and its purpose. They opened many doors and found many gifts in the space of their mystical friendship. Eventually, the teachings led to an experience of being co-facilitators of Dream Weaving Workshops and beyond. What follows are their collective dream stories.

Note to Readers

The art discussed in this book is displayed on the following websites:

www.ShamanicDreamtime.com

And

www.KellieMeislDreamArt.com.

Foreword
By Roberta Ossana
Editor, *Dream Network Journal*

Dream Stories: Recovering the Inner Mystic reveals a unique and ever-evolving friendship between the authors, Connie Caldes and Kellie Meisl, that spans two decades. They have known and supported one another through the best and most difficult of times: marriage, the birth and raising of their children, divorce, breast cancer, death and more.

In the beginning, theirs was a relationship born of a common challenge explored in Robin Norwood's *Women Who Love Too Much*—and it flowered over the first ten years. At that juncture, they began sharing their dreams with one another and the friendship has been/is enhanced and deepened dramatically. They began living *the symbolic life* in earnest.

Dream Stories, chapter by chapter, contains accounts of each of their personal and often shared experience. Courageous sharing into the depths of their joy, pain and all levels of human and extraordinary experience in between.

Their sharing covers a range of limitless dream experiences—both sleeptime and waking dreams—from warning dreams and nightmares, healing, precognitive, synchronicities, shamanic dream experience, shapeshifting, reincarnation, visitations from the other side, to lucid dreaming. Authentic sharing that is often embellished with poetry and art. With each sharing is an account of what was transpiring (or about to transpire) in their lives and how their dreams assist and guide them along the way. Often, the revelation of the meaning of each of their dreams results from their mutual dreamsharing.

This wonderful book is filled with encouragement and techniques for each of us.

Forward! Come along on this powerful journey.

Introduction
An Initiation: Removing the Mask
By Kellie Meisl

Dare to live the life you have dreamed for yourself. Go forward and make your dreams come true.
—Ralph Waldo Emerson

It is December 1998, and for the past several months, I have been walking regularly and doing some healing exercises I call *Meditative Walking*. I have been discussing the meaning of dreams with my friend Connie. It is all new to me; another aspect of my life is beginning to unfold unexpectedly. I receive an initiation into this new dimension through a dream experience:

Removing the Mask

I awaken in my dream; it is pitch black. The only thing I can see is the face of a beloved family member whom I lie next to. It is covered with a white encrusted mask. I am alarmed. I know this mask needs to be removed. I reach over with my right hand to pull it off. It will not budge, yet I know I must not give up. I finally loosen it and as I begin to remove it, an invisible entity pierces my right hand with large needles that I cannot see and only feel. I am afraid but I know I must remove the mask. I pull very hard, ignoring the sharp piercings and I remove it.

Two days later I sit with my spirit teacher; she is a wise woman from whom I seek counsel. I tell her my dream. "You performed the work of a shaman," she tells me. "What is a shaman?" I ask...

Chapter 1
Shamanic Dreamtime: Discovering the OtherWorlds
By Connie Caldes

I do not know how to distinguish between our waking life and a dream. Are we not always living the life we imagine we are?
—Henry David Thoreau

The shamans of indigenous cultures consciously traveled the *dreamworld* to heal individuals and ensure the survival of their communities. Resurgence in this ancient wisdom indicates that our culture is opening to the gifts of dreaming and the many benefits of listening to dream wisdom. Personally, working with my dreams has taught me much about my inner being and the need to listen to my heart.

For many years, I have known that dreams were guiding me in making choices. Dreams of long-lost friends prompted me to look them up. Terrifying dreams demanded that I make major changes in my life. Dreams of deceased loved ones eased my pain during difficult periods. Precognitive dreams surprised me. And, mystical dreams left me in awe.

I thought that everyone dreamed this way, with deep emotion, vivid color and powerful content. I think everyone does. Some do not remember. Some do not want to remember because they don't like the message contained in these dreams. Others have been told that dreams are nothing more than random nerve firing and consequently, they discard them as useless. But many believe that there is much more!

We are a confused culture when it comes to understanding the purpose and meaning of dreams. Are dreams communications from our soul? Is it possible to extract guidance and wisdom from our dreams? Can we find creative solutions to complicated problems (including those that are technically challenging) in our dreams? Albert Einstein spoke of his dreams guiding him in his work on Relativity. Do we work out our everyday issues in the following night's spontaneous dreams?

If you have come to believe that you might be more than your physical body, I invite you to consider working with your dreams as a means of exploring your spirit. There are many ways to do this, but it is best to begin by keeping a journal. And, if you don't remember your dreams, state an affirmation just before going to sleep and write down something when you wake, even if it is a feeling or thought. Begin to send a signal to your deeper self that you wish to lift the veil between your conscious and sub-conscious. In recording my own dreams, I've found that I have many types, a few of which I will share here.

A profoundly healing dream came to me in 1999 in which I perceived myself to be outside of my body:

Child in the River

I wake up to find that I am floating above my bed and facing upward. A card comes through the ceiling with a light blue angel inscribed on it. I realize that I am free of my body and wish to stand on the floor. I am transported to the desired position with sensations that are somehow familiar to me. I pass my hand through the curtains and confirm my ghostly status. A river forms in the floor of my bedroom, under my favorite window. As I look into the river, I am surprised and somewhat fearful because I see a little girl struggling in the current. I realize that this little girl is my younger self. Birds appear in the window behind the river.

This dream has had life-changing consequences for me. First, the sensations of being outside the body during a dream were beyond exhilarating. For me, they confirmed that we are so much more than our physical selves. Next, I did everything within my power to further explore my childhood and the meaning of this image. This process has been deeply healing and has guided me in discovering gifts that I might bring to my friends and community. And finally, the dream compelled me to learn about shamanic healing, which has led me to many enriching life experiences and even new work.

I have had many lucid dreams in the recent years and find them to be exciting. A lucid dream is when we *wake up* in the dream and realize that we are dreaming. Here is an example of such a dream.

T-Rex Attack

I am running from a T-Rex. Suddenly, I become fully aware that I am dreaming, feel fear flow out of my body and turn to face the T-Rex. I punch his snout repeatedly until he turns into a non-functioning blob. Then, he re-emerges from the blob and goes after me again. I attack him again and he is reduced to another blob. This time it is really over. I am very pleased with my power and that I did not give in to fear.

When I woke from this dream, I was acutely aware that the attack was an illusion. I strive to reconnect to that deep knowing when other fearful situations arise. Also, I felt sad when I thought about this dream and wondered if the T-Rex might have had a message for me. When I used a technique to go back inside a dream to search for more information, I heard the T-Rex say "Slow down!" My immediate thought was that this was a commentary on my life-style, but soon after, I received a speeding ticket. In looking back in my dream journal, this was the second time that I received a speeding ticket right after dreaming of the T-Rex. The T-Rex might be more than a metaphor for a police officer with a radar detector, but I will be checking my speed whenever the T-Rex shows up. And, as usual, synchronicity was about to strike. A few months later, I was driving down a road and noticed a large green construction vehicle. The side indicated the brand as *TeRex*. My foot went for the break pedal immediately as I assumed that I was getting a warning. Just one mile later, on what was a very rural road sat a police officer pulling over unsuspecting drivers.

We can dream of departed loved ones. In the late 1980s, I had a series of dreams about the wishes of my grandfather who died in 1975. I will discuss these dreams in detail in a later chapter. The dreams centered on my father and his love of baseball. I felt profoundly guided and supported by my grandfather in these dreams. Many months later, I found myself sitting in the movie *Field of Dreams*. I was blown away by the strong connection between the story in this film, my family history and the dreams of my grandfather. At that time, I could not make any sense of how I could have dreamed the themes in this film prior to its release. These things still surprise me when they pop up, but I don't try to understand. Rather, I know that it is confirmation from the otherworld that our waking reality is limited, and that we are not limited to it!

I wake up in a state of awe when I dream of reading poems or hearing music. This dream was one of my favorites:

African Chorus

A friend and I take a ride to the ocean. A group of people, African except one Asian male, in gorgeous colorful gowns, walk toward me on the shore, singing a beautiful African song. I hear sophisticated harmonies in a foreign language. They pass me, turn and face me and sing more. An African man in his fifties leads this group.

6

The vivid sights and intricate sounds in this dream mystified me. I felt honored by the chorus of beautiful people. A little more than a year later, I found myself working with Malidoma Some, author of *The Healing Wisdom of Africa*. It did not surprise Malidoma or me that he looked very much like the man that led the chorus in my dream.

I sometimes see beautiful ethereal visions in my dreams. They have an *otherworldly* feel to them. One showed up at a time when my husband had partial hearing loss and was being tested for a brain tumor:

Eagle Totem

I "wake" to a beautiful sight in my room. Near my husband's tall chest of drawers is something that looks like a totem pole, except it is ethereal, appearing to be made of a lightweight tissue paper-like substance with all sorts of filigree patterns cut out all over. On top, sits a beautiful pure white bird. In front of this totem-bird image is a swirl of energy and light rotating in a clockwise direction, like a spiral towards its own center. This image appears to be riding on the end of a light beam that is pouring in the window.

When I woke from this dream, my memory of the breath-taking image in front of my husband's dresser convinced me that he was not in medical danger. This feeling was soon confirmed when the MRI came back negative and his hearing returned. This dream is still my lifetime favorite!

I've learned from Sandra Ingerman, faculty member for *The Foundation for Shamanic Studies* and author of *Soul Retrieval* and *Medicine for the Earth* that from a shamanic point of view, power animals empower, protect and guide human beings. I dream of many species each month and notice certain animal images showing up repeatedly. As an example, I often dream of bears. Amongst Native Americans, Bear is the Great American Medicine Animal. For others, Bear is the Great Mother. When the Bear shows up in my dream, I honor the dream by working with it extensively, searching for messages of protection and healing.

Dreams of death are often frightening. Some people think they mean that they are going to die soon when these dreams might be pointing to part of them that needs to die to open to a deeper life. This is not to say that death dreams are never about physical death, but I've had two dreams of my own death, both of which directed me to terminate an unhealthy relationship in order to resurrect myself.

Synchronicity in many forms is a natural by-product of dreamwork. You will see the images, people, animals, symbols and more from your dreams show up in waking life in the most unusual of ways. You will know when it happens. And those that believe in the magic of the universe will be receptive to your stories. Your relationships will be more exciting if you share your dreams and synchronicities.

There are many gifts of the dreaming. Dreams can help you recover lost aspects of yourself, find your soul friends, discover your life's work, deepen healthy connections, find the courage to end destructive relationships, write with greater creativity and be in touch with your inner guidance. The gifts are endless. Set intentions when you go to sleep. Ask questions. Look for answers. Your life will change! May you find your own majesty! And may you have wonderful dreams!

Song of the Deer
By Connie Caldes
Written on 1/10/02

Reaching for the clouds,
Winding as I climb,
Infinity abounds,
Entry to the worlds.

Artemis, my companion,
Dancing by the river,
Moonlight lit lagoon,
Garden of the night.

Chapter 2
Soul Healing: Walking the Walk
By Kellie Meisl

Walking is man's best medicine.
—Hippocrates

I began to walk everyday during my pregnancy to maintain my physical health. When my son Benjamin was a year old and I had been at home with him for that year, my reasons for walking became much more conscious and therefore, so did the way I live my life.

On the sunny days in fall of 1998, I began to listen to a tape series as I walked. Listening to tapes devoted to human consciousness was a practice I did every morning to prepare for my work as a teacher. Walking and listening together was a new exercise for me. Walking is a naturally balanced exercise and incorporates both hemispheres of the brain, so the combination of walking and learning worked well for me. Sometimes I would walk and listen for an hour or more while my son slept peacefully in his carriage. The first series I listened to was Caroline Myss' *Energy Anatomy*. It had a major impact on my thinking. The information she shared made it glaringly clear that *how we use our energy—and allow our energy to be used—has everything to do with the life we have.*

Shortly after listening to Myss' series several times, I began my own inner process of healing work. I started to direct my energy in a focused way with intention. I understood the concept of deliberately focusing attention toward clearing energy to produce a desired result from listening to Ester and Jerry Hick's *Abraham Basics* series. It introduced to me such

1

concepts as *Law of Attraction* and *Law of Deliberate Creation*.[1] What came to me naturally were exercises in cleansing, healing and recreating myself through identifying my energy centers and focusing upon them. The exercises have a physical composition to them because I am directing my energy toward my physical body—and physically walking while doing them. They also have a cognitive component because I am unplugging from outdated belief systems that no longer benefit me, and I am creating new mental spaces for a different way of thinking. I am bringing in new thoughts and ideas with intention. The exercises contain emotional elements because I work with my feelings, allowing them to surface, experiencing each as it comes to me. The exercises are spiritual in nature because I am examining all of these processes to discover my highest good, my *Reason for Being*. I am surrounded by spirit *in* nature while I am performing them as well.

As I walk and tune into all of the aspects of myself, I place an intention while I am navigating through each layer that any stagnant, harmful, or pent up energy that I possess will dissipate into infinitesimal tiny particles. I ask that this energy will then flow in a rhythmic way through the channels where it is contained and keep moving. I also take care to send this energy in millions of directions so that harmful energy is not released back into the world. When I begin my focus on my physical pathways, I may be feeling pain in an area of my body or a general fatigue that needs to be cleared. Or, I may just scan my body allowing the areas of heaviness and undesired energy to be revealed to me. Similarly, when I focus on my emotions, if an unresolved issue is producing strong feelings, that may be where I place my intention for resolution, but I also make space for emotions to surface freely. I work on the cognitive aspect of

---

[1] Esther and Jerry Hicks, *The Law of Attraction: The Basics of the Teachings of Abraham* [CD] (Carlsbad: Hay House, 2006).

myself by honing in on my thoughts. When I do this I may be working on changing a belief I have taken on that no longer serves me, or I may want to clear my mind to create open-minded space for new thoughts for a new project I am doing. I find working on changing thoughts and beliefs requires a lot of awareness and attention. Thoughts of all kinds need to surface unconditionally and be acknowledged as they are let go of. I work on matters of spirit by tuning into my dreams and to the natural world.

Blocked energy can take on various forms including physical, emotional spiritual and cognitive. It may manifest physically as in the experience of illness. Stagnant energy may affect spirit; this happens when one experiences blocked creativity or a lack of purpose in life. Energy blockages show up in emotional forms too. We see this in the high incidence of depression experienced in our culture. Stale energy may manifest cognitively as attention deficit disorder or a learning disability. Of course there are layers within layers as a spiritual crisis may also induce depression and depression may lead to physical pain and so on. Always, as I work with energy, I have the underlying intention to disperse any blockage by changing its form, allowing it to flow, and healing the area by sending pure energy, in the form of light moving through me.

One of the specific ways I work on removing blocks and healing old wounds is by doing an exercise I call, *Cleansing the Pathways with Healing Light*. As I mentioned, sometimes I have a specific focus on an area that feels blocked, other times I discover where energy is blocked as I move through the exercise. For this exercise, I envision energy in the form of cleansing and healing light traveling through me. The light often takes on different qualities spontaneously, such as color. I identify my physical channels, where energy travels, as I go along: my brain, synapses and nerves; my heart, blood vessels, and blood cells; my bones, muscles, tendons, and ligaments;

and, my glands and organs. It is helpful to look at an anatomy book to get a general idea of the inner workings of the human body. But it is not required, as generally tuning in helps you to get a sense of where things are located. I then go through my chakras, whirling energy vortices, beginning with the chakra at the base of my spine or root, my navel, my solar plexus, my heart, my throat, my third eye, my crown and ending with chakra above my head, which I envision to be my connection to divinity. I name each area, sending and feeling the cleansing light while it is releasing the blocked energy, and allowing it to be transmuted. A wonderful book for understanding the basics of chakras is *New Chakra Healing* by Cyndi Dale.

I perform this exercise for about a half an hour, envisioning each part of my whole being, the pathways and channels of my body, my emotions, my thoughts and my spirit, acknowledging each area, one at a time, removing blocked energy, then sending light. As the light moves slowly through each area, beginning in my head and feet simultaneously, I see and feel the light meeting in my solar plexus and intertwining along my spine. Then, the upward moving light continues traveling up, through my hands, arms, heart, throat, head and above, while the downward energy continues down through my abdomen, hips, legs, and finally my feet and into the Earth.

It is in my third chakra (solar plexus), the energy center of personal power, where the light intertwines in my cleansing exercise that I focus on my emotions. In a process I call *Community of Emotions* I allow all of my feelings to surface: anger, sadness, fear, joy, calm, confidence. I envision the emotions together in one *space* located in my solar plexus. I begin with the predominant emotion that is with me in the moment. Each emotion is given its time for expression; I feel and embrace each emotion. I thank the emotion for its purpose, for its contribution to the whole. I then envision each feeling connecting to its counter-emotion to provide a harmony. Often,

I find myself operating on only a few emotions. By bringing in the full spectrum of emotions, I achieve balance.

Tuning into my physical body and my emotions will often propel me to other areas I am working on in my life. Many times issues of how I am relating to the world around me will become the focus. I recognize that relationships, whether between two or more people, people and places, or people and things, are an entity of their own. Relationship to *things* might mean my relationship to time or money for instance. This concept is well explained in Neal Walsh's first book, *Conversations with God*. His chapter on relationships has been invaluable to me. Therefore, I realize that it can be effective to send love and positive thoughts to the constitution of a relationship. While performing this exercise I call *Rainbow Ribbons of Light*, I envision my relationship in need of healing contained in a glowing, blue sphere of light. I place an intention that all harmful beliefs or thought patterns that are held within this relationship be removed and healed. I take time to acknowledge the beliefs or thoughts that surface, and then let them go. The blue sphere of light acts as a protective environment where the relationship can heal and maintain its pure essence. From within the protective sphere, I extend loving thoughts using rainbow ribbons of light as a visual. They gently flow between and around the other being and me. If I am focusing on a relationship to a thing such as time, I extend out each ribbon with a positive thought such as time flowing freely, or always having enough time. I envision a never-ending continuum of time that spirals and flows rhythmically. Each ribbon is my gift to the relationship, my offering toward healing, toward connecting in a purer way. Eventually, these beautiful rainbow ribbons of loving thoughts and visions are encircling "us". They undulate and swirl. I allow myself to absorb the love and place an intention that the entire entity of the relationship will absorb the love as well. Since I do not attempt to heal others without their consent, my intention is simply around healing the relationship I am in with others. As Neal Walsh states about relationships, "Let each person in relationship worry not about the other but only, only, only about the Self."[2]

Around the time I was going full force with what I call my *Meditative Walking*, a synchronous event occurred. I began studying dreams with Connie. She too was a stay-at-home mom, home with her son who is just one year older than mine. We had been friends for ten years by this time, and began talking on the phone, mornings, while our sons napped. In no time, our conversations turned to the topic of dreams. We had both experienced lucid dreams in our lives as well as many significant dreams we each held in our memory that dated back to our childhoods. Connie recommended I read Richard Bach's series beginning with *Illusions,* followed by *The Bridge across Forever* and *One.* I read them while she reread them and our daily phone conversations turned into book discussions including the lucid dreaming aspects of the Bach stories. Bach believed in the power of dreams and of a parallel universe where one might be able to visit an alternate aspect of oneself. I also gave Connie the *Energy Anatomy* tapes to listen to. My focus turned to working with my dreams with more intention.

The most life altering lucid dream experience I have had came six months after I began discussing my dreams, while I was performing my *Meditative Walking* exercises daily.

Rainbow Swirl (March 18, 1999)

I awaken in my dream. I feel my entire body vibrating intensely. I can feel every part of my body from my head to my toes all at once. As I open my eyes, I see white light

---

[2] Neal Donald Walsch, *Conversations with God, an uncommon dialogue* (New York: Putnam Adult, 1996) p. 124.

shooting through my body in sync with the vibrations. I hear celestial music playing. It is a soft rhythm with an "other world" quality. Then I see a swirl of rainbow colored light come toward me and undulate above my solar plexus. I observe another rainbow swirl above the African violet plant on the table at the foot of my bed. I look at the window beside it and see the blinds are raised though they were closed before sleep that night. I can only see darkness through the window. I try to rise toward the window but cannot. I realize I am meant to stay with the light. The light and vibrations feel very healing and I decide to direct them to my solar plexus. This sends little pinpoints of green light, which enter one at a time along my c-section scar. I then close my eyes and see bright green light in my mind's eye. I also see a dark tunnel with the outline of a human form falling through it followed by a series of symbols, which I do not recognize, except for a pyramid.

I then awaken in physical reality with my hands *still vibrating*. I realize healing energy is contained within my hands. I know this healing energy is valuable and I do not want to waste it. I immediately think of giving this healing energy to my husband who has just been diagnosed with diabetes three months ago. We have been working together to find healing for his disease. Because it is late, and I do not want to wake him, I make the decision to re-enter the dream state and fly to him to send him this healing energy. I am able do this with ease.

I fall back asleep and float out of my body to my husband Steve. I hover over him as he sleeps. I can see him clearly. He is lying on his back. I place an intention to send him the healing energy. Ruby colored light with gold flecks flows through me and into him through his entire body starting at his head.

This astounding experience altered my view of the composition of life. I now believe that our waking physical reality merges with other realms of reality—including the dream world and that we have access to these other realms. It is a matter of directing our energy with intention and focus. It is also a matter of having awareness. I believe the swirling rainbow light that was above the African violet plant at the same time it was above me, was showing me the *nature* of spirit and the connection between all living things. I am sure that my *Meditative Walking* exercises prepared me for this dream experience. In many ways those exercises came alive in my dream.

Coincidences in my life now grab my attention more readily. My dreams often merge with physical reality. I now see waking life as a dream, a waking dream, full of metaphors, synchronicity and serendipitous events calling to me, inviting me to explore their meaning.

Focusing my intention has changed my awareness dramatically. Working with my energy and bringing my attention to wellness has healed my life in a dramatic way. I am far clearer on how I live my life and, I am grateful to be walking this walk.

Walking,
A Metaphor for Life
By Kellie Meisl

Slowly,
slightly clumsily,
I move.
Flickers of crystals cling,
to the skin,
wrapping my ankles and feet.
Nature's breath burns my cheeks,
blows through me.
A dim golden ember, sends a faint welcome warmth,
to my bones.
Thickly layered Earth supports me,
Her sharp edges pleasingly dulled,
Her dark places tenderly swathed,
lie sleeping now,
tossing and turning,
in the life of their dreams.
Temporary hills and valleys,
settle themselves,
into an imposed yet harmonious relationship.
My body winds rhythmically with
some effort to keep my stride and balance.
Energy of Nature's elements,
moving through my own elements.
I open my containers.
I am
on an old familiar path,
with a
sacred new beginning.
Walking,
a metaphor for life.

Chapter 3
Creativity Heals: Releasing Old Patterns
By Connie Caldes

We must be willing to get rid of the life we've planned, so as to have the life that is waiting for us.
— Joseph Campbell

Six years ago, I was initiated into the world of cancer when I found a lump in my breast. The lump was positioned such that it did not show up on mammography. However, since I found it myself, I went to a surgeon and had it removed and subsequently found out that it was breast cancer. This was a very traumatic experience for me, but since I detected the tumor very early, I was spared a mastectomy and chemotherapy. Instead, I chose to have a lumpectomy and radiation treatment. I feel blessed to have had the options offered me by early detection. It is my hope that many other women will have those options. This is more likely if women check their breasts monthly and go for their annual exam and mammogram.

After the diagnosis, I was in absolute despair for many weeks, unable to take in all of radical changes that were happening to me in both my medical and personal life. And, despite the fact that many wonderful family members, friends and medical personnel supported me through my crisis, there were those that just did not understand the magnitude of trauma that one feels after a breast cancer diagnosis. From some, the message was "get over it." Unfortunately, this sentiment is often expressed far too early, long before the patient has finished treatment and begun to heal on physical and emotional levels. In fact, I read in *Hope Lives: The After Breast Cancer Treatment Survival Handbook*, by Margit Esser Porter, on this issue: "Some people have actually asked me why I can't just put this *breast cancer thing* behind me and get on with my life. As if I won't be truly healed until I can abandon the subject. I want to tell these people that if I were an alcoholic and needed to go to AA meetings three times a week, they'd applaud my courage and my goal of sobriety. But this disease, this breast cancer, which was not self-inflicted, has it's own serenity prayer: God grant me the serenity to tolerate idiots!"[3] I whole-heartedly agree!

I personally found an outlet for my feelings in the early weeks after the diagnosis by writing poetry. The following poem was my first:

Breast Cancer Descent
By Connie Caldes

Alone in the darkness,
surrounded by those who do not comprehend
the grief that is mine
in this journey to the underworld.

Searching for meaning
in the midst of despair and confusion.
Who to turn to?
Answers escape me.

Healing is tangible
when just a concept,
much more daunting
if the stakes are high.

Bodily trauma,
surgery, drugs and treatment,

---

[3] Margit Esser Porter, *Hope Lives: The After Breast Cancer Treatment Survival Handbook* (Peterborough: h.i.c. publishing, 2000) p. 38.

difficulty calming the mind,
reaching to grasp the soul.

Exploring death,
I thought that I was too young,
children and husband,
preempted life's work.

To the guardian spirits,
show me the new path
so that I might rise
and walk in the light.

I found peace and healing in journal writing, yoga, organic cooking and working with my spontaneous-night-dreams. The writing provided an outlet for painful feelings. The yoga and organic food helped me find my center and get my body into good shape, which resulted in a sense of well-being. Working with the symbols in my dreams gave me keys to healing my past and re-directing my life down a new path.

Within six months of the diagnosis, I felt worlds better, no longer plagued by constant terror that the breast cancer would return. I let go of things in my life that were no longer top priority, and did only the things that I love the most. I found many new friends in my healing journey through breast cancer and am grateful for the deep sharing that has been part of my life in the wake of the diagnosis. In many ways, my life was just beginning. Peace and joy return if we express our feelings and the desires of our souls.

I encourage all women who have had a breast cancer diagnosis to reach out to other survivors and to allow the emotional pain to be channeled through creative endeavors. This might include writing, artistic projects, taking walks in nature, singing healing songs, pursuing support networks or exploring a heartfelt desire that has been put on the back burner. Once you have had time to regain your balance, try to go back in the world and express the creative being that you are. The mask of having to please others has been lifted because cancer teaches that we cannot afford to waste time with false facades or unsatisfying relationships. The moment to find peace, love, and healing is NOW.

Afraid of the Afraid
By Connie Caldes

I had cancer
It's gone now
All gone
I think
I know
I think
I'll never know
Then I get scared
I am afraid
I am afraid of the cancer
I am afraid to die
I don't want to leave my children
I want to live
To stay here
To have another chance
To seize my life
To develop my work
To dream
To write
To have fun
Go to movies
See the world
And then I get scared again
This time I am not just afraid
I am afraid of the afraid
Some people say that if you are afraid of it
It will come back
And then I wonder
How can I not be afraid?
This disease has come
It rocked my body, mind and spirit
It hit like a ton of bricks
A nuclear bomb

The scariest thing I have ever heard
You have cancer
Oh my God
Me?
And now after hearing that
You tell me
But don't be afraid
Because if you are afraid
It might come back
Well screw that!
You see how you feel
If someone tells you
You have cancer
Yes, you see how you feel
And then you might be more sensitive
Sensitive to the fact that
We can't just will our fear away
It's a trap
If you are afraid
Then you will make yourself sick
Well, that is quite a bind
For the most grounded of humans
So, how do I solve this dilemma?
I tell myself the truth
I am afraid
Then I work with the story of the afraid
Then I tell myself another truth
That afraid story is a story that does not need to be.

Chapter 4
Casting the Heroine: Healing From Breast Cancer
By Connie Caldes

It was told me in a dream
That I should do this
And I would recover
— Algonquin healing song

As I shared in Chapter 3, In March of 2002, I was diagnosed with Breast Cancer. It swept into my life and gave me a shock that set me on a new path, a path I could not have imagined, and a path that would bring my dreamwork into greater focus.

I had many initial questions. Why did it come? What had I done to bring this upon myself? Why had I not fully considered its possibility in spite of warnings? As an example, sixteen months prior to my diagnosis, in November of 2000, I dreamed:

The Retirement Party

I am in a large room with two female friends and dozens of men. It is a retirement party for a man, seemingly from General Electric, a place where I had worked. The tables and chairs are dark and dingy. I feel bad that I do not have privacy to talk about an issue with one of my friends. I am on the periphery of the room. SUDDENLY, toward the center of the room, a young man is frantically spraying green Windex on himself and throwing hunks of bread. There is a feeling of chaos and impending doom, possibly an invasion, attack or nuclear bomb. I suspect aliens. Then, a BOOMING male voice comes over the loudspeaker and says, "I am sorry to announce that on September 30, 1994, you will die of cancer." The announcement is for everyone. I wake terrified.

When the surgeon told me that my tumor was malignant, I entered an unfamiliar world. I sat in his office with my husband, Michael, and a friend and felt excruciating emotional pain.

Bone Scan Day
By Connie Caldes

Two days ago, I found out that I have breast cancer
Today, I am having lung X-rays and a bone scan
They want to see if the cancer is in my lungs or bones
Those are the places that it often spreads to
I take a deep breath while they take the X-rays
Now I breathe deeply, in a state of ANXIETY
What will those pictures show?
Am I OK or am I dying?
They move me to the bone scan room
I lie down in the tube
The equipment flows up and down over my body
Scanning Scanning Scanning for twenty minutes
Searching for SPOTS on my bones
They may be under attack
Oh, I pray that this is not so
METASTASIS!
Oh God, please don't let there be any of that!
Let my lungs and bones be clear
Please tell me that I will live
Relax, you will be in the tube for a while longer
Meditate
Breathe
It's over
I stand up
My legs are weak with terror
Scan results showing on the computer screen
He looks at me out of the corner of his eyes
Is he trying to hide what he sees?

I analyze everything
I try to read the technician
I think that he is worried about me
ANXIETY takes over
I can't breathe
I am gasping
I want my results
But I can't have them
I go home in despair
I can't sleep
WAIT WAIT WAIT
Then they might tell you
IF YOU ARE GOING TO LIVE

"How can I turn back the clock? How can I possibly tell my children? Does my cancer nightmare mean that I am going to die?" I struggled for about 48 hours in immense despair and then received an unusual gift.

I asked for a sleeping pill, and my doctor who knew that I did not take mood-altering medication lightly, honored my request. He gave me Ambien, in low dose. According to Michael, a few minutes after taking the pill that should have put me to sleep, I sat up in bed and announced, "I don't know where I am!" Michael tells, "You then curled into a fetal position and shook for ten minutes, repeating that you did not know where you were."

When the shaking subsided, I sat up and looked around what was a very different bedroom. I saw fuzz balls in the air, bright points of light on the walls, and most interestingly, energetic waves with little people emerging from the bouquet of flowers on my dresser. I asked Michael, "Can you see the little people?" Bewildered, he answered, "No." This was confusing to me because the experience was vivid and intensely alive. I moved around the room, gazing into the bouquets at close range and took note of flowing stamens in the lilies. Everything in the room was in a kind of slow motion. I was in awe of *life*.

With great difficulty, Michael eventually convinced me to go to sleep. When I woke the next day, I felt transformed by this walk between the worlds of waking consciousness and sleep. I had dreamed while awake, and I had the feeling that I had released some trauma. This was a departing from an old life, a death of sorts.

It was months later when I realized that prior to this profound vision, I had been focusing on the image of a hummingbird for healing. During a workshop at The Omega Institute, while journeying to the shamanic drum, I received a message from my guidance: *Your experience with the flowers was perceived through the eyes of a hummingbird, a perspective that reveals the unseen miraculous world in the life of a flower. We have opened your vision!*

A few days after the vision in my bedroom, I had the following waking dream:

The Spider's Web

I am looking out of my kitchen window and see a large spider injecting its venom into a beautiful dragonfly that is caught in its web, a web that is skillfully attached to my hummingbird feeder. I relate to the dragonfly. I realize that I am entangled and that I need to free myself. I remove the dragonfly from the web as the symbolic act of freeing myself from anything that drains me.

I subsequently terminated several unrewarding relationships. The natural world had sent another communication to help me re-direct my life. Shortly thereafter, I read in Jean Shinoda Bolen's book, *Close to the Bone: Life*

Threatening Illness and the Search For Meaning, on those diagnosed with serious illness: "It may be that they (finally) ended dysfunctional, soul-draining relationships with narcissistic, controlling, needy, abusive, or chronically angry people, who responded in their characteristically self-absorbed fashion to the news of the life-threatening illness."[4] It seems that most cancer survivors that I speak to can strongly relate to this experience.

Lumpectomy and Lymph Node Dissection
By Connie Caldes

As I entered the hospital that morning
That dark morning
I felt a wave of shock and terror consume me
I am about to have a NUCLEAR shot injected into my breast
wound
So that the doctors can track my sentinel node
They do this with no sedation
So I took an Ativan before arriving
A man approaches with a large needle
And I find the courage to say "NO!"
"I need to have a woman."
She arrives with a gentle smile
And speaks to me with kind words
She injects the substance
I breathe a sigh of relief
They place me in an open tube, a scanner
To watch the substance drain to my lymph nodes
Aha! They see the sentinel node
And take a picture for the surgeon
This is good news!
Because the surgeon might now find this node

---

[4] Jean Shinoda Bolen, *Close to the Bone: Life Threatening Illness and the Search for Meaning* (New York: Scribner, 1998) p. 41.

And remove it from my body
And if this node is negative for cancer
Then other nodes are likely to be clean
They roll me into the surgical waiting area
Where I lay on a stretcher for three hours
The surgeon is delayed with the patient before me
Complications, not a good feeling
Is that nuclear stuff still working?
Shouldn't they be injecting the blue dye now?
The surgeon comes out to speak to me
He says that he is confident that we should proceed
As I enter the operating room
The lights blind me
Large disks of bright white light
I feel as though I were on a spaceship
A specimen for their anatomical experiments
I can't wait to be put out of my misery
"Please get the anesthesia now!"
The deep sleep comes soon
Then I wake in recovery
Pain
Pain in my breast
Terrible pain in my arm
What has happened to my arm?
Pain killers
Many
More
Please
More
I am rolled to my room
Moved to my bed
My husband looks scared
I get settled
It is late
I don't sleep well
They wake you if you do

Nausea!
I vomit midnight blue
The blue leaves my body
I still vomit
The surgeon returns
Breast tissue is clear!
Two sentinel nodes!
Both clear!
Seven other nodes clear!
Gratitude!
I stay a second night
I feel better
Time to go home
Time to heal
Time to find out if I need chemo
Hopefully NOT!
Time to learn about radiation
A definite!
Time to start Lupron shots
Instant menopause!
Time to take Tamoxifen
"I hope I don't get uterine cancer!"
Time to eat better
Organic food!
Time to exercise
Yoga!
Time to write
Poems!
Time to cry
Floodgates!
Time to live again
Resurrection!

Prior to starting radiation treatments, I explored a guided imagery tape by Belleruth Naparstek. In deep meditation, when Naparstek said that a beautiful being would come and direct healing light to a wounded area of my body, I experienced a vision of a dolphin sending light into my chest. Chills ran up and down my spine, and I knew that I was responding to this image on a many levels.

After finding the healing dolphin, I held this vision during radiation treatments, constantly reminding my body that it was healing. This calmed my mind when the dinosaur sized radiation machine BUZZED at various intervals and helped me to accept my seven weeks of daily treatments in a state of gratitude and grace.

Radiation
By Connie Caldes

They say that it doesn't hurt
But your skin will turn red and itch
They say that it will heal the breast cancer
But it might give you a different malignancy
They say that you won't be sick
But oh, the fatigue
They say that you get used to it
But that high tech BUZZ always threw me
Laying there on the metal table
Breathe, but don't breathe
If you breathe too deeply
The beam will hit untargeted tissue
If you hold your breath
You will eventually breath too deeply
So, relax
Hold still
Close your eyes
Imagine
Imagine a loving beam of light
Entering your body
Soak it in

See it healing your cells
Maybe it comes from God
Or the stars
Or a spirit guide
Or the ocean
Or a favorite animal
It doesn't matter
Just hold the image
Visualize healing
Breathe softly
Comfort yourself
And soon
Soon the BUZZ will cease
Then you can sit up
And go home
Until tomorrow

Endeavors that brought me further serenity included yoga, reading, writing, connecting with other survivors, listening to relaxation tapes and engaging in artistic projects. As a student in the *Foundation for Shamanic Studies Three-Year Program*, I had been instructed to make a mask to honor an animal of my choice, the Deer. This mask was to accompany a dress that I had already created. With the assistance of a wonderful artist, Fern Leslie, I painted the mask and embellished it with meaningful objects. I found myself joyfully absorbed in the process. I was beginning to resurrect myself through creativity and return to the light with the fruits of my descent, an experience of living life close to death.

unWANTED Email
By Connie Caldes

Yesterday, I received unwanted email
The woman who wrote it requested healing prayers for others
And she listed their names and ailments

She said that one just had a lumpectomy and now needed a
mastectomy
She said that another had recurrent bladder cancer
And another had lost a breast only to now lose the other
She said that one had recurrent rectal cancer
She said that another had non-Hodgkin's lymphoma
And another had clogged arteries

Email like this is hard to take when you have just been treated
for cancer
So I closed the email window and got depressed
Yes, it put a damper on my day to say the least
I wasn't the same
First, I was refreshed from a nap
Then, I was in despair over cancer recurrence

Such are my emotions these days
They swing from one extreme to the other
I am OK, then, I am not OK
I am relieved, then, I am frightened
I love my life, then, I am thinking death
I feel healthy, then, I am afraid I am sick

And, so the pendulum swings
Exhausting, frightening, confusing
Life in the wake of cancer
Life interrupted
Life re-directed
Living life close to death

Then, I asked the Universe to show me how to move on. I sensed that I should sit and be in my body, listen to the birds, paint the vision in my mind, write whatever came to me and be with my children. These became my priorities. Soon after coming into greater alignment with my soul in this manner, I dream:

The Hummingbird Flies

I catch a hummingbird that is trapped in my house. I notice that he is bleeding near his beak. His feathers are vibrant. I want to put him in our parakeet cage so that he can heal. I place him in the cage and step away. Later, my son comes along and lifts the cage off of its base to clean the bottom. At this point, the hummingbird escapes to the outdoors and flies away. I am sad to see him go but relieved that he can fly.

I was excited about this dream because hummingbird was my image for healing. Months prior to the dream, I sent a drawing to Dr. Bernie Siegel, author of *Love, Medicine and Miracles*, in which I depicted a hummingbird removing a wound from my heart, near the site of my tumor. Then I had this dream of the little bird with blood on its beak. I inferred that the hummingbird was showing me the wounded aspect of myself. I was glad that I was able to give him a contained space to heal and that he flew away at the end of the dream. He was healthy and free, as I wished to be. He was showing me the way to fly on the wings of my spirit, to seek ultimate freedom from my past.

A few nights later, I dream again:

The Lumbering Bear

I am sitting in a forest. A large male bear lumbers by and shows no interest in my presence. I watch him as he vanishes into the distance.

In many of my dreams prior to the diagnosis, bears pursued, growled or behaved in an otherwise aggressive manner. Those dreams felt like warnings. In this dream, the bear simply marched on as if to say, *all is well here.*

37

At times, negative thoughts and scary visions would return. I found that writing poetry about anything that bothered me was the solution to releasing this kind of pain. I wrote poem after poem on every aspect of my surgery, treatment and other troubling issues. After that, if I started to feel any negativity, I was also able to released unwanted thoughts and images through yoga, visualization and art. One kind friend said that when I had scary thoughts, I could say to myself, "That is a story that does not need to be."

In the months that followed, my night dreams pointed out progress, how to continue on a healing path and issues I needed to address. In addition, the dreams provided images from the past that reflected the origin of significant issues, helping me to understand the deep impact of old traumas upon my psyche. Working with these dreams and images guided me in finding places where deepest feelings and needs were expressed, heard and treated with the sacred respect that they deserve.

One night, as I drifted off to sleep, I held the intention, "Show me the next step on my path." Then, I dream:

Sacred Attics

I am living in my old apartment where my bedroom was in the finished attic. There is a new master suite on that floor in addition to the original bedroom that I used in waking reality. I now sleep in the new master suite. As I enter the room where I used to sleep, I see a set of three tall, sleek and graduated bookshelves against the far wall. The three modular sections are three different pastel colors, turquoise, pink and sky blue. They are held together with a kind of gauze and they are also bolted with different colored, over-sized crayons along their sides. The shelves are covered with books and treasures from my past. I notice carpet in two textures, in various shades of yellow, green and blue. I am talking about having relationships with aliens, including with a male "cling-on" that I no longer see. I am in a support group for people who have also befriended aliens in the past. I create a junk pile of mostly plastic items. I want a library elsewhere in the house, but I decide to leave the shelves in my old bedroom and create a wonderful space there

I felt that this dream was instructing me to find a creative way to manifest a sacred space in my home, a place for my books and treasures, a place to gather and dream. I also wondered if this was about writing a book. I saw the aliens and cling-on as the people that I had shed from my life. The crayons and colors in the shelves and carpets seemed to comment on my new adventure with watercolors and a new sense of creative grounding. The gauze reminded me of material used to create my Deer mask, a message to continue to incorporate art. Purging the plastic reminded me of letting go of things that were not real, including people with false facades. The dream directed me to move ahead with my own creative work in my own safe space. I have since created that sacred dream room in two consecutive homes where I display and share my costumes, masks, art, treasures, books and spiritual materials and teach shamanic dream classes.

Shortly after a positive visit to my oncologist, I had a dream that set a new stage and made it clear that I was not only healing, but also transforming:

Watching the Transformation

I am in a room with several friendly doctors, including my oncologist and radiation oncologist. They are shining a diffused yellow light, which illuminates the inside of my chest and watching what is going on inside me while making many positive comments. It seems that what is going on inside me is magical.

The dream felt like a message that all was well inside of me and that a powerful transformation was in progress. I felt blessed.

About a year after my diagnosis, I made a second costume and mask, this time to honor Hummingbird. As I placed the final embellishments on my mask and felt the healing that the process brought me, I put out a question to the spirit of Hummingbird, "How can I bring this healing to others?" To my surprise, I received an immediate answer: Create an artistic cast of your breasts. *Paint and decorate with your personal healing images! Do it now!*

Within a week, my breast cast was complete, with pink lily and hummingbird painted where I had my lumpectomy, rhinestones placed over my lost lymph nodes and a golden dolphin as a tribute to the healing light of radiation.

This process allowed me to go deeper into my healing from the cancer, so I decided that I wanted to bring this opportunity to others. I developed a workshop for breast cancer survivors, *Casting the Heroine*, that includes dreamwork, shamanism, intuition, journeys to discover healing images, poetry, group sharing and creation of healing story breast casts. I brought my idea to the Women's Imaging Center in the local hospital and was told that a grant would be provided for me to do this work with women in my community. I taught participants how to create their own healing casts and felt elated that my life's work was manifesting. The breast casts from this workshop later became the centerpiece for on ongoing annual art show to raise awareness about breast cancer in our community.

In returning to my nightmare, *The Retirement Party*, I have reflected upon the many symbols and truths conveyed in that dream. Jeremy Taylor, author of *The Living Labyrinth* shares "Dreams do not come in the service of the ego or in support of denial and repression. They come to connect us more consciously to the deepest and most profound energies of our lives. The psychospiritual wholeness that dreams reflect and promote is much more complete and authentic than the sense of *conscious self* that is defined (and limited) by the waking ego."[5] In keeping with this belief, the dream spoke of many patriarchal issues that needed my attention, addictions and toxins that had touched my life, situations that I had experienced that were out of control, threats from the outside world and much more. Was the reference to "invasion, attack or nuclear bomb" a metaphor for invasive cancer (as mine was called) and subsequent radiation? I have spent many hours working with this dream, and what I find most intriguing is that the dream was accurate in that I did metaphorically "die of cancer."

What the dream did not share, probably because I woke in terror before it's resolution, was that I would be reborn into a richer life and once again find my way to the light, a much brighter light than the one that was apparent to me prior to my diagnosis. Cancer was the gift that brought me to this more meaningful and creative place. I would have it no other way.

---

[5] Jeremy Taylor, *The Living Labyrinth: Exploring Universal Themes in Myths, Dreams, and the Symbolism of Waking Life* (Mahwah: Paulist Press, 1998) p. 48.

Tamoxifen
By Connie Caldes

I had breast cancer
So I take Tamoxifen
They say that it blocks those estrogen receptors
And thereby prevents future tumors
They say that you must take it for five years
To have lifetime protection
But they also tell you
That it might give you uterine cancer
But they say that uterine cancer is curable
So better to get that
Then a nasty recurrence of breast cancer
Oh, what we have to do to stay on the planet

Lupron Shots
By Connie Caldes

They give me shots of Lupron
To end my feminine cycle
To put me into menopause
And say good-bye to youth
They say that if you have had breast cancer
It is better to stop the bleeding
Hormonal balance leads to
Better survival statistics
So, now and then I go to the clinic
And have an intra-muscular injection
It makes me sick for a day or two
But that is how I buy my health
And, oh, the hot flashes
I drip from head to toe
Sometimes every hour
So after months of daily soakings
I decide to take Effexor
Another drug, but who cares
The hot flashes are disrupting my life!
"I need relief!"
The Effexor works nicely
And takes a big bite out of the sweating
Leaving me to enjoy
Most of my waking moments
And especially my dreamtime
Allowing me a state of peace
So that I can go on
And try to have a normal life

Chapter 5
Waking Dream: Finding The Lost Little Girls
By Kellie Meisl

Hope is a waking dream.
— Aristotle

My husband Steve and I, along with our three and a half year old son Benjamin, pile out of our SUV. We meander across one cement square of a sidewalk, and in unspoken agreement, begin to stroll along the very green, slightly long summer lawn in front of a red brick apartment building-once school. I pause to notice its former name etched in the grey concrete above the bricks: "Johnson School." I stand, admiring the sturdy front door, crafted with character. School buildings just don't have that same appeal as they used to, I think to myself.

We walk across a solid cement bridge with thick posts and rails with little windows in between them. Below lies murky water with glistening spots of sun shining here and there. We are approaching a playground on the other side of town. Though I had always thought of this as a tough neighborhood, the park and playground are surprisingly bright and cheerful. Benjamin and Steve chose to come to this park, as they have been here before and really like its atmosphere too.

As I enter the park, I see several teenage boys playing basketball on red and blue courts, meticulously painted with white stripes and geometric designs like none I have ever seen on a basketball court before. Benjamin strolls happily along the edge of one of the three courts. The teen boys, intent on their game, do not notice him. One teen male sits on a bench taking a break; I want to say hi but we do not make eye contact. I get a feeling of positive energy as I walk through. We reach the playground equipment. It too is brightly painted and neatly kept. I expect to find graffiti but see none.

Several children, their skin a beautiful palette of ambers and browns, are playing on the climbing structure. They vary in age and size. The young boy is loud and high with energy, jumping a good four feet from the top of the slide and landing like a cat in the wood chips below. The girls eye us but continue playing within their tribe. I sense toughness about them and start to feel anxiety. I move in towards Benjamin and watch him keenly as he asserts himself, climbing up a ladder causing one of the girls, slightly older than him, to back up. Then, crawling through the tunnel, he meets up with the loud boy and successfully passes him without incident. I comment to Steve on his confidence level and begin to relax and let go of my anxiety. Steve and I walk over to a bench and sit down.

Benjamin goes over to the youngest girl there, barely a toddler, and tries to take the steering wheel out of her hand and claim it as his own. This makes Steve uneasy and he begins to call firmly from the bench at Benjamin to "give the wheel back to the girl." I tell him to ease up a bit. "You handle it then," he tells me. I go over and try to balance the situation and bring some harmony to the situation, avoiding negativity. At first I am unsuccessful at getting Benjamin to open up to the idea of sharing the wheel. He is about to turn four in a month and very much into his *me* phase of life. Steve keeps calling me to remove him from the area but I refuse to give up and soon the situation is resolved, with Benjamin even agreeing to share. The little girls are gathered around, each taking turns looking in on the youngest one, though she is well on her way to being able to take care of herself. I ask her name while I am playing peacemaker. "My name is Erica," I am told. "I am one." Soon I have the middle sister's name. "Glenda, five years old," I hear her say through a slight speech impediment.

They are *beautiful*, deep brown, their skin shining radiantly, spirals of black curls neatly collected atop their youthful heads. Glenda is wearing sky blue eye shadow. Though it is meant for someone many years beyond her age, she dons it as if it were tribal face paint; it serves to only further enhance the innate beauty of her face and skin. I soon realize the girls are friendly as they begin to share more and more about themselves. Glenda just finished Head Start; she'll be going to Drake Elementary in the fall. Another slightly older girl appears, her skin the color of autumn honey. She is wearing a fuchsia pink top and ruffled skirt; very pretty, impractical as playground wear, but it's her style and it suits her. Her eye shadow perfectly matches her outfit. She is, "Heather, seven," and she goes to Drake Elementary. Glenda shows me how she can cross the bars, swinging to two bars before jumping off. Heather proudly crosses all of them. Soon Glenda is asking me to hold her while she crosses the bars, which I do without a problem; her body is light, almost ethereal. Erica, or "MooMoo" as her sisters affectionately call her, wanders off to another piece of playground equipment—so does Benjamin with Steve in tow. I stay with the girls. Heather wants to be held now while crossing the bars. Her cousin, Glenda's older sister, reminds her that she doesn't need help but that doesn't stop her from taking it. Heather and Glenda retreat to two toddler swings. Their bodies, though very long for the swings, slip into them with ease. They beseech me to push them. I do so without hesitation, their free spirits, their friendly, welcoming attitudes, and their innocent beauty captivating me.

Soon they are talking about family. Heather's sister, more elusive, in a form fitting dress that ties in the back, looking to be ten, remains in the background. We are introduced but her name doesn't stick. Glenda reminds me that she lives at 309 Milton Street and has five sisters and two brothers. Heather tells me she has ten sisters. With Glenda, I get a sense of pure truth. With Heather, I feel the need to read between the lines,

47

yet I know there is truth in her words. She tells me about a brother who died in her mother's stomach. I tell her that's very sad. They continued to be delighted as I push them on the swings; they attempt to keep their turns fair.

They are most pleased by my attention; I feel completely calm, and my spine tingles with the sensation of peace. This is what life is: pure reality, a spontaneous trip, a chance meeting, youthful—(albeit on the brink), feminine energy. Ahhhh. I look to Steve and receive an acknowledging smile and am even more comfortable in the place I find myself. This is the simplest and best day of our weeklong vacation so far and it's Friday.

Soon Isaiah, Glenda's brother, wants to swing. He comes in with a tough masculine attitude that threatens to break up our powwow. My feelings of wellness permeate his surge, however, and soon he is allowed to share the swing of his cousin, Heather. Erica has wandered over and been placed in Glenda's swing. I'm back to holding Glenda on the monkey bars but glance peripherally at Isaiah, picking up on his need for support in this whir of feminine energy. I go over and push him on the swing, which magically penetrates his defensive barrier. Through his disturbed speech, I hear how he can dive into a "dar" (pool), and about his burnt rabbit that died in the fire that was set in his home and in which he lost everything except his Barney. His cousin reminds him that the rabbit now carries a burn mark. I make the suggestion that Barney is somehow special and can be held for comfort. He doesn't shun the idea. He continues to talk of fire and lighters and how he can light them and firecrackers. Sierra, yet another cousin, comes over to push MooMoo, inserting details into her brother's tales in a most respectful and mature fashion for a ten year old whose birthday will be on August 7th. I mention how special it is to have a summer birthday. She too is receptive to my input. Isaiah gets off the swing to go see the rabbit, a muskrat, which runs away at the last moment he approaches it. He comes back and happily reports that it went into the water. It hits me, using the Native American ritual of working with power animals, would be great for Isaiah. He then threatens to punch Heather who is now occupying his swing. Both she and he know that he means business; she leaves promptly. When he returns to the burnt rabbit in his conversation, I take the opportunity to ask him if he is sad about the rabbit. He proudly retorts, "No, I laughed because it bit anyway." I decide not to judge but to just stay with him in his story; this works out well. He tells me about his brother who lives in Philadelphia and who called yesterday to ask for a picture. He mentions his Dad is living there too. Wishing I could send him an animal totem, I ask him for his last name. There is some confusion about this and both he and his cousin decide on Judd Daily—that's his father's name, he tells me.

Then Steve calls me. "It's time to go to the hardware store before it closes," he tells me. I tell the kids, who are still vying for my attention with an intensity that tells me they are not yet filled up by my interest, though they are sincerely delighted by it. Sensing my impending departure, Heather asks quickly, "What's a hardware store?" I blurt out something about nuts and bolts and tools. Isaiah asks if there are toys. Heather wants to know if they have notebooks. "No," I tell Isaiah. "Maybe," I tell Heather. She imploringly asks if I'll buy her one; she needs it for friends' addresses and "to write about friends and stuff." She asks if I could bring it back today or meet her here tomorrow. I ask her what her house number is. "Twenty, I think," she replies. I will try to find it. Then I stroll, with Steve and Benjamin back to our vehicle, mesmerized by the richness of my experience, still vibrating from it all. The question that has become my mantra of late: *What is my life's purpose?* pops into my head. As I cross back over the bridge with the glistening river beneath it, I smile with an inner knowledge that I am receiving my answers. Something is swirling beneath us there in the river; *it's Isaiah's muskrat*, I think. As we reach the green lawn of the brick apartment building-once school, I ponder: *What color notebook will I get for Heather?*

I consider this experience to be a *waking dream* because, like spontaneous night dreams, it is one of those times when every thing moves in varied time frames. Although the physical body is moving in linear time, the emotional body is moving in dream time, rather like a lucid dream with an edge on having abilities that help you perform feats of an emotional nature rather than those of a physical nature, such as willed flying, which we may associate with lucid dreaming. A waking dream can merge one's mind's eye with the present experience at hand and the gifts can be profound. One receives the aptitude to look at his or her life in past tense, present tense and future tense all at once. One also gains a sense of what we now know is so crucial to mental health, the absolute, power to really *live* in the moment.

What spurs these waking dreams? Aside from the fact that we are all receiving these experiences regularly as we go about our day, though we might not be aware all of the time, I believe taking the time to work with our night dreams helps. Doing so opens new doors for each of us to begin to look at our life as one big dream. Just as we can journal about, confer with others on and receive guidance about our night dreams, for the purpose of bringing us clarity about our mission in life, so too can we treat our waking lives in the same manner. So, we can journal about our waking experiences, confer with others about them and use dream techniques to bring clarity to them.

One dream technique that can help us gain understanding about a waking dream experience is Dream Mapping. The Dream Mapping technique works particularly well with waking dreams. With this technique, one places a particular theme from his or her dream into the center of a piece of paper. For this waking dream, I use the theme: "playgrounds". Then, I brainstorm any feelings or associations that seem connected to the central theme. (I might include: "an area of open ground" or, "a place where I left parts of myself as a little girl"). Each new piece of information is written around the periphery of the central theme. Lastly, I connect the main feelings and associations that resonate most with me by drawing a line first from the central theme, and then to each important word or phrase. What emerges is a visual and written "path" that provides more understanding about my waking dream. Just about any dream analysis technique one could use to learn more about spontaneous night dreams, can be used for waking dreams.

It has been almost three years since I wrote my waking dream story. I have found *myself* to be the one writing "about friends and stuff" like Heather had hoped to, as I weave my dream stories together. (I did return to try to find her but I never saw her again, I hope she is writing anyway.) My female relationships have become more of an integral part of my life. I am working with my friend of fifteen years, Connie, developing this book. We hold dream circles and workshops together monthly. We just returned from Nova Scotia a month ago where we held a weekend workshop for twenty women, ages eighteen to sixty. This experience brought us closer together and put us in touch with the intimacy of our friendship. Often times that weekend we found ourselves transmitting thoughts and ideas to each other without using verbal language. We could incorporate them at the spur of the moment into our work as facilitators, finishing precisely where the other left off without missing a beat. I have rekindled a childhood friendship with my birth friend of 40 years, another waking dream story that I tell in the pages ahead. Over the summer I sat weekly, sometimes for hours at a time, slumped in comfort, sipping coffee and pouring out emotion with my former teaching partner and kindred spirit for the past eight years. We have learned that we are more the same than different. I commented recently the story she just told me could have come out of my mouth instead of hers. "The lines between you and me have blurred," I tell her. Being with my friends has taken on a quality of play. I find myself telling my friends I love them more freely. Is this in part due to my waking dream experience on that summer day? I think so. It is with deep appreciation that I thank this waking dream for reuniting me with the lost little girls. For, I am a grateful dreamer.

Chapter 6
Planes, Dreams and Eagle Feathers: Dream Flight
By Connie Caldes

Flying may not be all plain sailing, but the fun of it is worth the price.
— Amelia Earhart

I am flying over my hometown in the passenger seat of a four-seat plane with Bob Berman, friend, astronomer and author of *Biocentrism, Secret of the Night Sky* and *Cosmic Adventure*. We soar with a gentle grace that feels like an old friend. The Berkshire Mountain range appears small with rounded hills, and I cannot get my bearings. Then I spot *Onota Lake*. "Go that way! My house is over there!" We swoop over the house and my children scream with glee in the back of the plane as we look down at our small spot on the planet. Oh how I wish that I could do this each day. Flying, what a feeling!

I don't have this type of waking experience every day, so it is not surprising that it would give way to wonderful dreams. The next night I have two dreams of interest:

Facing the Wind

I am with Brenda, a friend from childhood. We are in our childhood town. We have a discussion about needing to take flight and start jumping into the air to see if we can maintain lift. Someone points out that it works better if one leans into the wind. Brenda and I face the wind and leap into the air. We are lifted into the air and maintain our position about one thousand feet above the ground. I am thrilled with my skill and enjoy flying with Brenda.

Brenda and I had lost touch for a few years, but we had recently spoken on the phone. At that time we discovered that both of us had traumatic experiences in the past two years. I felt that the dream was telling me that we had risen above the issues in those respective traumas and that we would enjoy spending quality time together in this post-traumatic period.

Golden Eagle Gift

I am walking up a hill and notice a large kiosk to my left. I see a Golden Eagle and its silky white baby. The baby seems to have adult form, but I know that it is young because it is white. I continue to walk up the hill and eventually turn and face downward. Then, the Golden Eagle flies past me, from back to front, brushing against my cheek and leaving a pile of Golden Eagle Feathers for me in various sizes. One feather is uncharacteristically long and thin with blue highlights. I feel excited about the feathers!

Golden Eagle Gift was an exhilarating dream. In waking life, I love birds. I cannot wait for the day that I see an eagle in the wild here on the East Coast (I have seen them out west). But mostly, I love their feathers. I collect feathers and enjoy using them as healing tools. To receive many forms of the Golden Eagle feather was a magical experience in the dream. I woke longing for the feathers, remembering in particular the blue one.

Within a couple of days, I found myself gazing at a vase full of feathers in a home that I was visiting for the first time. I asked the owner about one feather in particular, to which he replied, "that is a Golden Eagle feather." So, I dreamed the dream and then for the first time in my life, encountered the feather. That's how dreaming goes, weird! This experience reminded me of another dream from many of years ago in which I received feathers as a gift:

Five Bald Eagles

I am at a friend's house, up the hill from the Omega Institute. I go outside and walk up the road to my right. I hear a ruckus in the sky and turn to my right. Way above, on my left, a hawk is chasing a crow and other smaller birds. The same is going on with a group of birds to my right. Suddenly, majestic white eagles with gray spots soar onto the scene (10 foot wing spans.) I refer to them as Bald Eagles. Their beauty blows me away. One eagle joins the group on the left. Four eagles join the group on the right. In the group on the left, either the eagle or the hawk eats the crow. In the group on the right, one of the four eagles eats the hawk. I am very surprised about the hawk's death.

The group of four eagles on the right lands on the ground and I approach them. I hear a voice in my head that says, "don't get near a Bald Eagle; they can take your arm off." I approach anyway. He threatens to bite, but I reach out with my hand and place it on his beak to calm him. He is as tall as my heart chakra. He threatens again but does not bite. Then, the four eagles fly away and I am left with the gift of an armload of dark Bald Eagle feathers (not the white feathers of these birds, but feathers of the physical Bald Eagle.) I am elated and excited about this gift. I know that I need to clean the feathers in water and share one with a friend.

The experience of physical flying in a plane had opened the door to new dreams of flight and triggered my memory of a flying dream from my past. Five Bald Eagles had originally come a few months prior to a diagnosis of breast cancer. In the shock and trauma of that diagnosis, surgery and treatment, I had lost touch with the gift of the feathers in my Bald Eagle dream.

But, the day before my breast **surgery**, several months after my dream, Kellie brought me a bald **eagle** feather. I will always remember what she said as she han**ded** me that feather to assist me in getting through my surgery, "Connie, you have to do this. I don't know what I would do without you." Intimacy comes when we least expect it, and thank God it is there to see us through our personal crisis. I was actually able to focus on how much I loved this gift instead of all of the difficulty I faced.

Kellie
By Connie Caldes

Kellie, my dear friend
Of fifteen years
My soul sister through
Many tough times
A powerful dreamer
Came to my side
When I was ill
Brought me an eagle feather
When nothing else would
Bring me comfort
Sent me food
When I was too hurting
To feed myself
One of the few
That was with me
In my despair
Stood by my side
When I was betrayed
Wrote a healing dream story
For my resurrection ritual
Sensitive
Honest
Dependable
Artistic

Intuitive
So true a friend

In the wake of a plane ride, flying dreams and healing from cancer, the memory of Five Bald Eagles brought me a sense of power with respect to my personal shamanic practice and inspired me to work with eagle energy more often. As soon as I vowed to do this, I started getting requests for shamanic soul retrieval work. Did the dream bring the feathers to me when I most needed them? Were Bald Eagles to be part of my personal healing? Were they to inspire my soul retrieval work with others? Were Kellie and I about to fly on the wings of this wonderful spirit together?

Many months before my plane ride, Kellie and I had planned a workshop for twenty people in Nova Scotia, On the Wings of Spirit. We had not been thinking of the Eagle spirit when we titled the workshop. But, I believe that the Eagle spirit was thinking of us! The wonderful feedback that we received from the people that attended our workshop has launched us into new work together. It seems that Eagle has become a shared totem for us, in every sense of the word.

The Bald Eagle feather sits amongst my treasures, a gift of a lifetime. I am thrilled to be back in touch with eagle medicine these days, dreaming of more eagles and placing totems of their images in my new *Dream Room*. They are majestic creatures that came to me in my dreams. All I need do is get on a plane or imagine their majesty and I am flying high!

To shift gears in my discussion of dreams, a parallel story that emerged for me during my day of flying with Bob Berman involves an old waking dream, a dream of my grandmother always telling me that my nose was too big. While dining with Bob at the Dakota restaurant in the Berkshires, I became uncomfortable when I realized that he seemed to be staring at me. At this point, he exclaimed, "Did you have a nose job?" Shocked by his question, I said, "NO! Why did you ask me that?" His response, "You have a perfect nose!" At this juncture, I drifted into a strange waking dream, a moment where I could not reconcile the beliefs of my past with what I was hearing from Bob. I was speechless, a rare state for me. The next time I saw Bob, I brought up the subject of my nose and the strange thing he had said to me. His reply, "Oh yes, I have been admiring your nose today, you have a perfect nose." And, when I emailed Bob to ask him if it was OK to quote him in this article, he replied, "Hi Connie. Yep, you can quote me anytime, and attribute anything to me whatsoever. And yes, your nose is definitely in the top 5% of the general population in terms of perfect noses." I am still trying to wake up from this dream!

Bob Berman came into my life while I was being treated for breast cancer and what FUN he has been. Eventually, I attempted to speak with him about my enthusiasm for dreams. I shared with Bob a wonderful technique for exploring dreams, a method that helps to uncover personal myths, taught by Stanley Krippner, author of The Mythic Path, only to hear him mumble, "Why would anyone want to do that?" I told him that getting in touch with personal myths brings our unconscious into consciousness, hopefully helping us to get out of our own way at times. Again he mumbled, but this time with an affirming nod, "OK." So, flying with the astronomer has brought me wonderful dreams and reflections, and maybe it gave Bob Berman a taste of the gift of dreams. At the end of Five Bald Eagles, I know that I need to share a feather. I have decided that Bob is the friend with whom I will share the dream bald eagle feather. After all, he did say that he would teach me to fly.

Chapter 7
Synchronicity: Making Amends with Ellen
By Kellie Meisl

I think we dream so we don't have to be apart so long. If we're in each other's dreams, we can be together all the time.
— Bill Watterson

Coincidences are a true paradox... on the one hand they seem to be the source of our greatest irrationalities--seeing causal connections when science tells us they aren't there. On the other hand, some of our greatest feats of scientific discovery depend on coincidences.
— Josh Tenenbaum

On June 17, 2002, I have a dream about my childhood friend. I have had dreams about her often, though I have been estranged from her for the past four years, a split I liken to the purging cycle an ocean goes through. We too have under gone the necessary purging cycle of any relationship that has lasted an entire lifetime, weathering the decades of early childhood, adolescence, and young adulthood right through the decades of parenthood. In the dream I call, *Making Amends With Ellen*, I am talking to her telling her I have had recurring dreams about her since we have been apart. I tell her I miss her. In the dream she tells me she too has had dreams of me. We decide to rekindle our relationship. When I awaken, I recall the dream and how really good I felt in it. I still feel good as I write it down in my dream journal.

On June 19, 2002, I am in our kitchen with my four and a half year old son Benjamin. It is the first of our summer vacation mornings, early, and we're preparing some lattes to take out on to the patio as part of our ceremony to welcome in the time we'll spend together this summer, blissfully unhampered by schedules and places to have to be. The phone rings. As is my typical fashion, I do not answer but let the machine pick up. Whoever is calling will most likely leave a message and I'll call them back when I have a chance. I do not wish to be encumbered by long conversations on this morning. Then, I hear the message. "Hi Kellie, it's Ellen, I'm in town with my little girl, sitting here at Irene's diner, had a moment and thought..." Instantly, without forethought, at least not in the waking world so to speak, I grab the phone. "Ellen?! I've missed you so much! Please come over for a cup of tea and bring your little girl!"

Needless to say, our relationship was rekindled on that day. The dream that I had of Ellen two days before her call led me to be prepared for this life experience. But, also, the *many* dreams I had of Ellen helped me to process my feelings about her and how much I valued her, without the interference of projections that surface so automatically in my head from day to day. I *knew* how I felt and what I wanted to say when I heard her voice.

Two weeks later, she came back into town with her husband, her two sons and her six-month-old daughter whose acquaintance I had just recently made. Her oldest son, five and a half, is my godson; he was just two when she and I parted ways. Her second son, three and a half now, was not even months old. She left our childhood hometown after being back here for a relatively brief stint while her husband served in the Navy. I didn't realize she had moved to New Hampshire until I got a note that she was pregnant with her third child, three months before she was due. I didn't realize how much I had missed her until she came back.

It is on a beautiful, sunny, summer day that we decide to trek the paths at a local bird sanctuary together with our families. We had all been to a Boston Pops Concert the night before and had a really nice time. She and I sit on a rock in the middle of the dense forest, off the trail and near a brook. Our sons run through the water in their water shoes, and stir water holes with sticks while our husbands follow closely behind. Is *this* a dream? We talk about family and friendship, ours, and how happy we feel together right now. Words and feelings flow more easily and purely than they ever have. Bliss. She tells me a story of the last time she had been here, how a massive number of Rose-Breasted Grosbeaks had swarmed into the nearby feeders in one of the fields at the sanctuary. We both agree how special it is to sight one of those beautiful birds—and especially to see a whole field of them!

The time we had spent together that weekend was truly healing in every way. The day she left, my heart was both filled with joy for the love we shared and sadness because she was gone again, albeit temporarily this time. That morning, as she was getting on the road to return to her present home, just after I had spoken with her on the phone, I sat at my kitchen table to have a cup of tea (that soothing, familiar pastime I had done with Ellen so many times) and reflect. Out of the corner of my eye, I spied a branch from my tiny crabapple tree buckle under the weight of a seemingly large bird. I got up from the table and walked to the back door to catch a better glimpse of this bird; it was a Rose-Breasted Grosbeak! Another synchronicity, a confirmation that yes, we are both on the same path *together* even in the physical absence of one another. Caroline Myss reminds us, in her tape series *Energy Anatomy:* "Your heart does not need geography to be close to someone."[6]

Later, I looked up the symbolism of the Rose-Breasted Grosbeak in Ted Andrews book *Animal Speak*; he writes that

---

[6] Caroline Myss, *Energy Anatomy: The Science of Personal Power, Spirituality, and Health* [CD] (Louisville: Sounds True, Inc., 2001)

symbolically Rose-Breasted Grosbeak can mean: "...healing [old wounds and hurts] of the family heart..."[7] Indeed, four years after being apart, Ellen and I had healed some of the old wounds and hurts that had caused us to separate. Reflecting on my dreams and the sequence events that took place that summer of 2002, I am sure of one thing: in dreams we can heal.

---

[7] Ted Andrews, *Animal Speak* (St. Paul: Llewellyn Publications, 1993) p. 148.

Chapter 8
Shock, Horror and Ghastly images: Healing Trauma

By Connie Caldes

Dreams are postcards from our subconscious, inner self to outer self, right brain trying to cross that moat to the left. Too often they come back unread: "return to sender, addressee unknown." That's a shame because it's a whole other world out there--or in here depending on your point of view.
— Dennis Koenig and Jordan Budde

Many of us have dreams that cause us to wake in terror. When they occur, the fear can be overwhelming. The dream does not feel like a friend. Why did I have that horrible dream? I often have asked myself that question. But after doing a lot of work with some of my nightmares, I believe that the dreams came to help me heal. They seem to point to the injuries of the past, at times from a bizarre perspective.

In the following paragraphs, I describe an early nightmare in my life and a series of nightmares that came in a cluster almost two decades later. I share the initial impressions from each dream, and toward the end of the chapter I share more recent insights.

In 1983, after graduating from college and living apart from my boyfriend, I had a powerful dream of death:

Lava Death (Early 1983)

I walk into my college sweetheart's dorm room. He is sitting on his bed. I move towards the stereo to play some music. As I attempt to place the needle on the album, everything begins to vibrate and the ground opens up, creating a huge hole that swallows the entire building. I realize that I am experiencing a massive earthquake and I try to flee. I find myself plastered against the ceiling, face up, as molten lava flows into the room. There is nowhere to go. In the last moment of the dream, it becomes clear that I cannot escape. It is all over. My muscles go limp and I relax into death. Then, a jolt of adrenaline surges through my body, and I wake with a pounding heart and unbearable terror.

I was in great emotional pain about this relationship for quite some time, for my sweetheart was pursuing his new life in graduate school elsewhere. The image of being eaten up alive by the ground and then suffocated by lava compelled me to pack my bags and leave the state in which I was living, waiting for my boyfriend's return. In looking back, I am certain that my dream guided me to pursue a more rewarding and less painful existence. At the same time, I was certain that there would be more to learn from this dream.

Many years after *Lava Death*, I had a two-month period in which I experienced several nightmares. The nightmares began in October of 2000 and persisted into December of that year. The first dream occurred while I was at *The Monroe Institute*, participating in a program meant to help access personal guidance. Well into the six-day program, I dream:

Wicked Woman (October 15, 2000)

I am with my husband, my son David, my daughter Tara, a wounded little girl that once harmed my daughter, my college boyfriend and a weird woman. The strange woman shoots my college boyfriend many times. The rest of us try to get away from her and end up in a room high up in a tall building. I leave the room briefly and when I return, the weird and strange woman says, "Where is David?" I am terrified and know that she did something to him. I am not sure if she has flushed him down the toilet, chopped him up, thrown him out the window or hidden him. I check the toilet and he is not there. I go downstairs to look for my son and the now wicked woman is in the street with a gun. Police arrive. I ask people to check the grounds because I believe that she might have thrown him out the window.

Upon waking from the dream, I initially realized that the woman in the dream reminded me very much of a woman that had been cruel to my daughter, a situation that had caused my daughter and me much pain. I wondered why my son was the possibly injured child in this dream. Did it have something to do with his age (four and a half at the time of the dream)? The reference to the toilet hit home since a member of my family had often told me that I was almost flushed down the toilet when I was born since I was a female. Clearly this had planted a bad seed in my mind and was still with me. But why was the woman in the dream so wicked? What was she trying to tell me? In what way was her wickedness a gift?

Shortly after dreaming of the wicked woman, I had another terrifying nightmare:

Don't Get Too Close to Predators (October 30, 2000)

I am at a gathering with hundreds of people. A T-Rex is to be brought down the street, restrained with chains on the back of a flatbed truck. I am concerned because some people are too close to the road, hoping to get a close-up view of the T-Rex. Captain Crunch and an unknown young boy are amongst them. When the truck comes down the street, the T-Rex reaches out with its neck and snaps up the young boy. Many women are screaming. I am horrified!

The synchronicity that surrounded this dream in its aftermath amazed me. It went like this:

Shortly after having the dream, I read Marc Ian Barasch's book, *Healing Dreams*, only to find a very similar dream of a T-Rex described in that book.[8] The man that had the dream in Barasch's book was diagnosed with a life-threatening tumor after his dream.

Approximately six months after reading the book, while attending yet another program at *The Monroe Institute*, I shared my T-Rex dream with a male friend that I will call Paul. He and I laughed about the T-Rex dream, specifically the image of *Captain Crunch*, an association from my childhood.

Then, six months later, I had what seemed to be an unrelated dream about a sniper in Virginia (before the real sniper began his campaign in that area). Upon analyzing my sniper dream, my friend Ed said that because my most major association with the state of Virginia is *The Monroe Institute*, he thought that a male friend of mine from the institute might be sick. Within twenty-four hours of his dream interpretation, I received an email that Paul (my friend from the institute) had a terminal brain tumor. I was shocked at how this story played out and feared that there might be more.

Six weeks after hearing of Paul's brain tumor, I found a tumor of my own in my breast. While leaning into a mammography machine, I looked down and noticed the brand name on the equipment – TREX. The blood drained from my face and I knew that my tumor was malignant.

To return to my series of nightmares, my T-Rex dream was followed by what I consider to be my ultimate nightmare. I have shared this dream and my analysis of it in other writing, but will share it again to cover new associations:

---

[8] Marc Ian Barasch, *Healing Dreams* (New York: Riverhead Books, 2000) p. 73.

The Retirement Party (November 20, 2000)

I am in a large room with two female friends and dozens of men. It is a retirement party for a man, seemingly from General Electric, a place where I had worked. The tables and chairs are dark and dingy. I feel bad that I do not have privacy to talk about an issue with one of my friends. I am on the periphery of the room. SUDDENLY, toward the center of the room, a young man is frantically spraying green Windex on himself and throwing hunks of bread. There is a feeling of chaos and impending doom, possibly an invasion, attack or nuclear bomb. I suspect aliens. Then, a BOOMING male voice comes over the loudspeaker and says, "I am sorry to announce that on September 30, 1994, you will die of cancer." The announcement is for everyone. I wake terrified.

In prior writing, I have shared how this dream may have predicted my breast cancer and more, but before sharing recent work with this dream, I would like to share one more dream that pointed to childhood trauma:

The Dead Head (November 28, 2000)

I am at a store and trying to remember the name of a rock band. Then, I am in front of the apartment of a childhood friend, Beth. Beth's brother Sam emerges and gives me a big hug. Then, he is on the second floor, getting a male body out of the floorboards. Sam emerges again, with a dismembered head. I become physically ill from the ghastly sight.

This was another dream that was surrounded by synchronicity. When I shared the dream with my husband, it turned out he had just made a reference to *The Grateful Dead* (hence, the dead head association) in writing that morning. Then, I went shopping in Albany, NY that afternoon. A particular store attracted me, *The Dancing Bear Trading*

Company, because of its association with someone that I knew. When I entered the store, it was full of *The Grateful Dead* paraphernalia, including many skulls.

When I considered the possibility of literal elements, I recalled that a man had committed suicide with a rifle (in waking life) in the apartment building in my dream, on the second floor, in a room that shared a wall with Beth's bedroom. Beth had heard the whole ordeal. Rumor had it that he had *blown his head off.*

Clearly, this dream wanted my attention. I would only find out years later a deeper truth of its call.

Four years after my nightmares, with no incidents of equivalent impact in between, including during my trauma with breast cancer, I read a book by Olga Kharitidi, *The Master of Lucid Dreams.* In her book, she travels to Samarkand to work with a dream teacher who shares deep wisdom about human trauma. Kharitidi is shown a technique for bringing images that evoke feelings into her perception in a new way in order to uncover the traumas from her past. She makes great progress with understanding what ails her and later, with healing the wound uncovered. This healing occurs with a conscious dream journey to address an issue that is terribly painful for her. Please read her book if you would like to learn more about the techniques and judge for yourself how to implement them in your dreamwork. I could not do them justice to describe them here.

While reading her book, I had a fascinating dream that showed me that the techniques described would be powerful for me:

Pure Essence (October, 2004)

I am in a mall, in front of a store, talking to a woman in a fur coat. I am telling her about the dream technique that I just read about in "The Master of Lucid Dreams." I sit face to face with the woman, close my eyes and begin to pull an image into my perception. An image of The White House grows more and more vivid in my mind and I begin to feel myself detaching from my body. Now I am my pure essence, floating above my body in a state of bliss.

So, I decided to perform the technique that requires bringing an image into perception from a different place in the psyche. It seemed to me that although Kharitidi had performed the technique on an image that had caused sadness in waking life, I would use terrifying images from these dreams to attempt to get at my deeper truth.

Upon returning to working with the *Lava Death* dream imagery, I was transported to a scene in my apartment during college. I had called my boyfriend and asked him to come visit so I could play a song for him. As I dropped the needle unto the album, Linda Ronstadt's painful rendition of *Long, Long Time* began to fill the room.[9] The song is about the trauma of having a loved one move away and more importantly about what felt like emotional abandonment. Upon remembering this time with my boyfriend, I fully understood why all hell broke loose in my *Lava Death* dream once the needle dropped onto the record. This image represented death in the form of abandonment and there was no doubt that I was in great emotional turmoil about it, hence the volcano and lava.

---

[9] Linda Rondstadt, *Linda Rondstadt: Greatest Hits* [CD]. 1976.

I then decided to focus on the *Wicked Woman*, only to find that a seemingly unrelated image came into my mind, an image of my cat Peanuts, hanging from a tree limb by a cord that was wrapped around his neck. When I was young, about the age of my son in the nightmare, I had tied a cord around my beloved cat's neck to take him for a walk. Peanuts had escaped with the cord still in place. My mother and I had then left for church. When we returned, my father was one hundred feet in the air on a ladder, rescuing my cat, *hanging* onto life in the tree. In my father's frustration, fear and anger, he screamed at me, "You hung the cat!" Although I do not remember the intense feelings that I must have felt upon learning that I had nearly killed my best friend, I am sure that I felt beyond devastated. The message of the dream became clear. I carry immense guilt. I am the Wicked Woman in my dream.

When I focused on the image of a T-Rex snapping up a little boy, an old scene faded into my perception, a scene where I had been *snapped* out of a door by a man and physically assaulted in the street as a teenager. I had been thrown onto the pavement and lay there unconscious with my head bleeding. When I woke, emergency personnel surrounded me. My mother was screaming in the background. And, just as the T-Rex was chained to flatbed, the man that attacked me had been very *attached* to his vehicle. It was very clear to me that this trauma had not been healed. Further, upon looking back at the time the dream occurred, I knew an individual who had similarities to the man who attacked me as a teenager. Since I had not connected the dream to abusive people, I did not heed the warning of the dream and later endured an unnecessary and disturbing encounter with that individual.

Although, I had done much work with *The Retirement Party* dream, I decided to dig deeper with the image of the threatening booming voice and its message. Although I did not get an immediate hit like the past trauma associated with the T-

Rex, two days later, I got my answer to this dream. While speaking to my friend Sue, I suddenly felt compelled to talk about a cult leader that had been active in Lenox, MA (*The Bible Speaks*) during the 1980s. I had heard an audiotape of him in which he told his congregation in no uncertain terms that if they did not behave, they would "get throat cancer." Sue said, "Connie, didn't you have a dream like that?" It hit me like a ton of bricks, "Yes!" My dream had made reference to something awful that I had heard in the past. And yes, the dream was warning me that there was a similar pattern playing out in my life at the time of the dream. Later, when I experienced the disturbing encounter that I spoke of above, there was no doubt that my vulnerable state in the midst of cancer was used for the purposes of control.

The next dream image I chose to explore was Sam carrying the head in *The Dead Head*. And again, although I had done a lot of previous contemplating, the old scene that would fade in was unexpected, an image of the father of Sam, approaching me in an inappropriate way at age fourteen. It was not as if I had forgotten the incident, it was just that I did not realize that it still ailed me and certainly had no idea that this dream was an anchor that would lead me to the treasure of understanding myself. I cannot emphasize strongly enough that the technique that Olga Kharitidi shares is one of the most powerful dream tools that I have discovered. I intend to use it regularly to heal my past and to discover my personal dream symbols. I cannot tell you how excited I am!

After writing all of the above, I went to sleep asking for a dream to help heal one of the traumas I discovered. I was not specific about which dream, but rather left it up to the spirits of the universe. Then I dream:

Basement Aviary (November, 2004)

I am in my basement inside a large, unfinished aviary. Some parts of the wooden frame and wire mesh still need to be constructed in order to safely contain the birds. Currently, two parakeets reside here. I am aware that many more birds will be added. I notice wood shavings on the ground to keep the area clean. These shavings will need to be cleaned out periodically. An unknown older woman points to the ground near the finished part of the aviary and says, "Look at that," affectionately. I see a small golden rat, hopping around in the shavings. The rat is petite and adorable. A golden mouse and a golden mole join the rat in what appears to be a loving and pleasurable conference between them. The mole has a long white nose, similar to that of an anteater. These ground dwellers are sweet, their color particularly enticing to me. Suddenly, from the unfinished side of the aviary, my childhood cat, Peanuts, the beloved cat that I had once hung by accident, appears in a casual manner. He is perfectly OK and happy to be with me as usual. I know that he needs to hunt, but I protect the rodents that are inside the bounds of the aviary. Within the aviary, there must be trust and peace.

In the short time that I have had to work with this dream, I see many healing images coming through. I believe that the dream takes place in a basement to symbolize the deep work that is going on in my psyche. The fact that the aviary (or safe container) is not finished shows me clearly that I have more work to do. I am intrigued by the combination of golden ground dwellers and creatures of flight that reside in the aviary, showing me that I must have my soul connected to both earth and sky in order to heal. The wonderful surprise of having *Peanuts* show up, letting me know that he is OK and that there is no more need for guilt was thrilling. When I woke, I could feel the energy of my beloved friend in my heart.

And just to confirm that healing was taking place, the following evening, the spirits sent confirmation in the form of a Chinese Fortune Cookie. The small strip of white paper read: *You will be free of the heavy burdens you have been carrying.*

I have been taking conscious dream journeys and continue to pray for healing for each of these early traumas in the hopes of laying my nightmares to rest. I am certain that with my dreamwork, creativity, prayers, zest for life and shamanic journey skills, I will heal these traumas and alter the "spirits of trauma"[10] (as they are called by *The Master of Lucid Dreams*) that produce fear and get in the way of our lives. I have already begun the process and the results have been rewarding.

Sweet dreams to all of you, and if they are not, work with them. They are the lifelines to our darkest and most painful secrets. It really is OK to have nightmares. We all have trauma in our pasts, and the nightmares show us where we need to heal.

---

[10] Olga Kharitidi, *The Master of Lucid Dreams* (Charlottesville: Hampton Roads Publishing Company, Inc., 2001) p. 41.

A Poem for Claudia
By Connie Caldes

*I wanted to write you a poem
in your style
even though I don't
write that way
so that you will know
you are not alone
in this difficult journey
through cancer*

*I don't know about the chemo
but I am with you anyway
because I hear your pain
in your poems
I feel sad about the very sick people
the moaning woman
and the children
especially the children*

*I had a different strain
of sorts
but the diagnosis was so
EXCRUCIATING
that I know how that part
feels
a nuclear bomb
a tidal wave
that you cannot stop
you cannot turn back the clock
and make the cancer untrue
it is there
it is there to heal
you must
if you love walking this planet*

you must
if you want to be with your loved ones
you must
if you want to come into full creation

I know that it is initially
unBEARable, but
we find our strength to
do what we have to do
to get WELL

We cry
we get depressed
we get angry
and then
somehow
the spirit cannot wallow
in all of that pain
at all times
and we find ourselves
enjoying the moment
the hour
even the day
then we know
we must do the work
to get well
no matter what

We are among
the lucky ones
we have a good prognosis
a second chance
the spirits are calling us
heal yourself
and
heal the world

Chapter 9
Dream Themes: Broken Teacups
By Kellie Meisl

Never to suffer would never to have been blessed.
— Edgar Allan Poe

In May of 2004, a series of events that caused significant impact in my life occurred. I wrote the following letter to my friends to share what I describe as a dream:

Dearest Friends,

What follows is a waking dream I'd like to share with you. Please read it when you have a chance. I welcome your comments.

Teacups

A week ago Saturday, I am sitting with my mother at her dining room table. Among other topics, we discuss the family china she passed on to me; it dates back to at least her great grandmother on her mother's side. She expresses her regret that four of the twelve teacups have been broken; she tells me that except for the teacups, the service for twelve is complete. She laughs about finding the lone sugar bowl top at an antiques store years ago and being happy to replace the only other missing piece aside from the teacups. I ask her to write a note about the set so I can place it with the set for posterity.

The next day, Sunday, I am sitting with my mother-in-law in her home. We discuss among many other things, china dish sets. She has just been to her eldest daughter's former home packing, packing and packing, she tells me, many sets of china dishes—literally hundreds of pieces among many sets which span the seasons decoratively. I mention I have but one set, a wedding gift from my mother, a gift to her from her mother that spans the generations.

The next day, Monday, I have come home from a day of teaching first graders. As is typical for me, I decide to organize my stress away. I open my china cabinet of ten years to place a miniature tea set on the top shelf with some other collectible miniature tea sets. The top shelf tips forward and the china from my great-great-grandmother that is on the first and second shelves smashes to pieces before me. I am shocked. I have never had a problem with the shelves in this cabinet in the eleven years I've had it. I bend to pick the pieces up; the crash has claimed the remaining eight teacups of the set as well as two dinner plates and a salad plate and has left the mark of a few chips elsewhere. I am so disappointed. One relief is most of the serving pieces: soup tureen, odd shaped bowls, gravy boat etc., have survived. I search the Internet for replacements, to no avail.

I begin to ponder the meaning of this waking dream, fascinated by the chain of events that brought me here. I bring up some associations I have for teacups. I note that Connie will soon get a teacup-sized poodle. I realize having tea is my way of socializing with friends. I wonder if there is a message here from my ancestors. I also note Mother's Day is nearing.

Switch to Friday, I write this an hour after my most recent development. Prior to this, I was organizing again, this time more relaxed, just the usual surface anxiety, or so I reason. I go into my china cabinet (please note, after the fall I made sure all shelves were stabilized, all brackets in place), the second shelf now gives way, smashing many more pieces, including most of my serving pieces. Amazingly, my mother's found sugar bowl cover survives. I am beginning to feel like the world is crashing in on me!

I would be grateful for any intuitive input any of you would like to give regarding possible meanings to this disastrous dream! I look forward to hearing from you.

Love,
Kellie

I send this dream off to my closet friends. I feel very alarmed by the abrupt crashing nature of the experience. Nine days later I write to my friend Cathy: "...when I do get a glimpse of a feeling, it feels like the destruction of the china is a mini-death; then I have to remind myself it's only china. I'm afraid for the other shoe to drop. Yesterday I came across *two* car *crashes* on my travels that had each just occurred, police not yet on the scene. This is one of those times when I don't feel like I have the full picture yet."

Indeed, I have been left with an unnerving feeling. Having inherited my belief in and fascination of superstition from my paternal grandmother, I fear a third thing will happen in this series of events; two shelves, two crashes, what is number three?

Cathy writes back to me with a list of possibilities that have "popped into her head." She shares with me that she looked up fragile in her dictionary. (This is a technique we often use for dream analysis: looking up a dream theme in a *regular,* not a *dream,* dictionary—it is astonishing how the literal definitions merge with the symbolic meanings of the dream.) She writes: "My dictionary lists under fragile: *that which cannot withstand even mild shocks or jars—e.g. a fragile **teacup!**"* The synchronicities just keep coming.

A week or so later, my Ellen and I have our usual morning chat on the phone over tea. After we hang up, the phone rings again not five minutes later. It is Ellen. "You're not going to believe this," she tells me. "The top glass shelf in my china cabinet just cracked in half, my teapot collection is suspended inside resting on the second shelf of china!" I ask her if there are any casualties. She tells me she is unsure and will call me back. She later confirms that all pieces have survived with the exception of the top of one pot, the one I recently gave her for a gift.

I then share my waking dream in the dream circle that I co-facilitate. Isabelle is a guest of our circle that night. She has just flown over from Germany for a visit. The input she gives me is very interesting. She shares that she had been reading *Excuse Me, Your Life Is Waiting*, by Lynn Grabhorn and therefore she was in touch with the concept of energetic resonance. Her intuition was telling her that the crash part of the dream had significant energy around it. Having read several books on the topic of energetic resonance including Grabhorn's, I understood exactly what she was saying and felt her hunch was correct.

However, all of the analysis I did with the help of so many intuitive friends could not have fully prepared me for the third event that occurred. Just two weeks after my original two crashes, a third crash would take the life of one of my contemporaries, a fellow teacher. In many ways we had lead parallel lives. We had both gone back for our teaching degrees as a second career and we graduated from the same college. We had both discovered early on that our true love was teaching and had insisted our siblings play school with us. She was Irish and her Dad was an Irish police officer. I am Irish and my Dad is Irish and was a police officer. We met only a year prior. She was my son's teacher then. We wound up having philosophical debates about education, sometimes labored, but we had worked on reaching a common ground. Some of that came from our life stories we shared. We gained a mutual respect for one another that wound up transcending our differences.

I saw her the last time on a Friday afternoon. She dropped a couple of her students off to play practice at the end of the school day. She drove her car to the edge of the grass, very close to where I sat on a blanket with a group of other students and my son, awaiting play practice. We made eye contact as she rolled down her window and we both wished each other a good weekend. We would have seen each other the next night at the school play. But that never happened. She was struck head on, on Route 22 only twenty minutes later and died instantly from a severe blow to the heart.

Blows to the heart can come in many ways. Life can sometimes seem so unreasonable and unfair. Like when your son has a rough year in kindergarten, or when the family china that has been touched by the hands of the generations of your mothers crashes before you. But those things really do pale in comparison to the seemingly unfairness of a valued human being's life cut short. I realize it is all about perspective. That is one of the big lessons I have taken from this.

There is another way that my dreams were linked to the teacher who brought me a lesson. Though she and I had had difficult times that year she taught my son, we had some high points as well. She had put me in charge of classroom parties. At year's end I helped host a tea party, in honor of the children reaching the letter T in the alphabet curriculum. The tea party was also held as a Mother's Day event. We dressed up; she wore the scarf I had given her as a gift and a straw hat. We drank from real china teacups. Everyone and everything looked so beautiful that day. We all had a wonderful time. She never forgot that day and would bring it up regularly when we passed in the halls the following school year. I am grateful for that, it reminds me that sometimes things that are broken can be mended; no matter how hard the lesson may be.

Now several months after the *Teacups* dream, I dream of the departed teacher.

Grace

We meet in the parking lot of the school she formerly taught at. We embrace and she tells me simply: "I am thinking everything you are thinking."

Is this confirmation that on some level we are all *One*? I believe it is.

Addendum: One year to the date of this story, I located replacement teacups for my great grandmother's set of china. I learned the china was made in 1941. The pattern of the china is called *Triumph.*

Chapter 10
Connecting to Our Roots: Greek Dreams
By Connie Caldes

Your descendants shall gather your fruits.
— Virgil

A new awareness of my heritage began in 1978 in my freshman engineering design course. I was partnered with a young Greek man (Chris, who later became my boyfriend) in a project. We were to design a method to remove a jack-knifed tractor-trailer from a bridge that was situated under an underpass, a difficult task to say the least for a pair of eighteen year olds. As it turned out, all of the design teams (except ours) suggested that one should remove the cab of the truck prior to pulling the trailer out from the underpass. But I knew better because I had interviewed NY State Police and was told that removal of the cab is nearly impossible in such situations. So, Chris and I did our best work to devise a solution that did not remove the cab while it was in the jack-knifed position. We were verbally rewarded for our persistence and design. We were told that we had won the *Apollo and Athena Award*. Was this an accident? At the time, I did not give it a thought.

A few years later, while working at my first engineering job, my co-worker Kay and I were disappointed when we forgot to send out invitations in time to have a Halloween party. So, it was time to get creative. We decided to hold a *Come As You Were In A Previous Life* party a few weeks after Halloween. The invitation, which depicted many ideas of how to dress (insects, famous people, animals, plants, etc.), read:

Come As You Were In A Previous Life

Who: You
What: A Party

Where: Connie's Place, Livingston, NJ
Why: Because You Only Live Twice

The party was a hoot! White people showed up as African Americans. African Americans showed up white. An amusing atheist came as a priest. A friendly democrat dressed as a republican elephant. Kay dressed as Van Gogh, with palette in hand, band aid on the side of her head and plastic ear hanging on a cord around her neck.

I had struggled with how to dress for my own party, and then the grandiose idea came to me. I thought, "well, I am a Greek, so I will dress as a Greek goddess." At the time, I did not realize how I would admire the images of ancient goddesses in future dreamwork, but I must have sub-consciously known that Athena was a meaningful force in my life; after all, I had won the *Apollo and Athena Award.*

My costume was easily assembled. A white sheet draped my body in the form of a sexy toga, gathered at the waist with a sparkling gold and silver belt. Glitter shown on all exposed skin. My hair was sprayed elegant and magical silver. I spent the evening feeling like a true goddess. This was the beginning of owning the archetype of Athena for me. I am only sorry that I did not carry an owl on my arm and place a snake at my feet!

I had to evolve a bit for a couple of decades before Athena would become important to me again. While reading the work of Jean Shinoda Bolen, *Goddesses in Everywoman*, I realized that I related strongly to the characteristics of the Athena archetype.[11] I certainly valued knowledge, and although I had

---

[11] Jean Shinoda Bolen, *Goddesses in Everywoman: A New Psychology of Women* (New York: Harper Perennial, 1985) p. 75.

already studied engineering, I was now attending a master's degree program in social work and informally reading everything that I could find about dreams, shamanism and human consciousness. It felt important to master many disciplines. I deeply wished to understand the human psyche. It helped to read books such as *Women Who Run With the Wolves*, by Clarissa Pinkola Estes, *Shamanism*, by Mircea Eliade and *Creative Dreaming*, by Patricia Garfield. I felt accomplished and expanded having read these great works and others.

But six months after beginning my master's and completing what was the beginning of serious dream study, I was diagnosed with breast cancer. I decided that I should leave school and my board work in the community to take time to heal.

Early in my treatment for breast cancer, and while attempting to further understand my life and current condition, I had a healing dream:

The Owl and the Pussycat

I am speaking with a Greek man who is holding a cat. The cat looks at me and says, "Calamatta." I comment, with some surprise, that the cat is speaking English. Then, a small owl descends from a glorious midnight sky and lands on my finger. I ask the owl, "Does this mean that I should go to Calamatta?" The owl nods in the affirmative. I ask the owl, "Is that because Yanni (the musician) is from Calamatta?" The owl agrees. I ask, "Am I related to Yanni?" Again, the owl agrees.

This was a thrilling dream for me. The gift of the owl descending from a magical sky left me with a multitude of positive sensations. It also brought me back to my Greek roots since Yanni's music always takes me there and the owl felt like a messenger sent by Athena herself. And although we are all related as a human family, I feel closely related to Yanni through my beloved grandfather who grew up not twenty miles from Calamatta. The dream let me know loud and clear that I need to travel to Greece, to the western coast, a small village known as *Pilos*. I have many relatives there and have made a pact with a German friend to explore Greece together. Frankly, I cannot wait!

Shortly after completing my cancer treatment, I have a wonderful dream of my Greek grandfather:

Visiting Papou

I am dreaming and realize that I am dreaming. I take advantage of this lucid moment. I decide to visit my Greek grandfather, Papou. I push through a thick black space and find him standing in front of a modern control panel, his coloring so intense that he borders on being a cartoon. He seems surprised to see me. I say "Papou!" I reach out and we embrace. The sensations of feeling him and knowing him again with all of my senses is so overwhelming, I wake.

When I woke, I was keenly aware of my grandfather's presence with all of my senses. It felt so affirming to see him and to know that he is still there for me.

Around the time of this dream, I went to an African shamanic workshop with Malidoma Some. A young man in the group was known for picking up on the spirits of ancestors with certain people. The minute that he saw me, knowing nothing of my Greek roots or the blue and white striped Greek flag, he announced, "there is a somewhat short and stocky woman with you, in a blue and white striped dress." I was shocked. I had always felt that my Greek grandfather was with me, but this confirmed that my Greek grandmother, Chrisoula, was present too.

I then decided to write a story about Chrisoula's life. On the very day that I decided to do so, I sat at my computer, eating a piece of cheesecake, perhaps the first time that I had eaten cheesecake in my home of two years. I had previously googled the phrase "Chrisoula Name," and found a reference to the name being a Greek nickname, Goldie. Surprised that her name was not related to Christine and rather to the Greek word Krysos, meaning golden, I again searched Google. This time, I entered "Chrisoula Name Meaning" and was startled to come upon the only website with information about her name, the website for "Chrisoula's Cheesecake." This certainly let me know that I was on the right track! Furthermore, after enduring seven weeks of radiation during May and June of 2002, I had gone on a one-year rampage of eating cheesecake every day. Upon reading the information on the Chrisoula's Cheesecake website, I learned that cheesecake was from the Greek Island Samos and that the Greeks fed it to the Olympians to help them gain strength. No one in my family had suggested that I eat cheesecake to heal and gain strength, yet I had been compelled to do so. My behavior had perplexed everyone in my life, yet they allowed me to indulge myself, as it was comforting at a traumatic time. Upon hearing this story, Kellie said, "Hey Conn, looks like your grandmother was with you all along, especially when you were healing from cancer." I am left to wonder if the owl in my dream was in fact my grandmother, calling me to Calamatta, a city very close to the place of her birth. And, I am left to wonder if our family name "Caldes" is related to "Calamatta."

In the wake of my Greek dreams, the spirits are still nagging at me about the importance of a trip. Over two and a half years after The Owl and the Pussycat, I had another dream of Greece:

White Sand

I am on a large cruise ship, with a navy blue hull and white upper decks. The cruise ship dispenses a large wave toward the shore. Passengers, including me, emerge from the ship and ride surfboards to the white, sandy beach. Once my feet have a chance to walk on the warm and soft sand, I realize that I am on the shores of Greece. This revelation is very exciting. I walk the shore for some time and come upon a museum or temple. A woman shows me an ancient statue of a disciple. I tell her that my beloved grandfather was from Pilos. At this point I sob for a great time over the loss of connection to my Greek ancestors.

Clearly, I feel deeply connected to Greece and her people. I only need get there to further expand my understanding of my heritage. Possibly, I will be more *disciplined* in my studies of ancient Greece, the Asclepian Dream Healing Temples that reside there and my psyche's alignment with Athena after my travels. For now, I will pay her (Greece) more visits in my dreams.

A final image that remains active in my psyche occurred in a dream quite some time ago. The vision was ethereal and somewhat intangible:

Heaven

I am with a young man on a beach. Far across the sandbar, I see a breath-taking place, ancient white buildings of mixed architecture. I tell the man that I am with, "that is where we will go when we die."

This vision reminded me much of the many photos that I have seen of the Greek Islands. I felt connected, comforted and certain about my choice for the afterlife. I feel assured that I have chosen a wonderful place to go when I decide to make my transition. Perhaps I will meet my ancestors there.

Chapter 11
Dreaming With Those On the Other Side:
Heaven's House
By Kellie Meisl

To die is to go and live in another home.
— C. L. Allen

I am in God's house. I am aware that a group of people will be meeting on the top floor in the outside courtyard. I will journey up a set of stairs to meet them. As I begin to ascend, I turn back and notice a pure white fresco; it hangs on the wall at the foot of the stairs. I try to focus on the picture that is on it so I can remember it. I see a design with bumps and holes in it but cannot make sense of what it is. I return to my journey up the staircase. I become aware that everyone attending the meeting above needs to bring a crystal. I do not have one and am concerned about this. Then, about half way up the stairs I look down and see a green crystal heart on the stair before me. I pick it up and notice there is a chip out of it. I wonder if I should keep this crystal to bring to the meeting. Instantly, I realize I must return it to its owner. I am filled with an inner knowing that I will not have to find whom it belongs to; the owner of the heart will be revealed to me. I know that I must wait and listen, when I hear the person's story I will know to whom the heart belongs.

I had this dream in March of 2000. It was one of those dreams where I *knew* it contained important information. In fact, I felt privileged to have this dream. I named it after a phrase my son Benjamin coined when we began to discuss death with him: *Heaven's House*. He lost his first loved one when he was age two, a beloved great-aunt named Tante Annie, his paternal grandmother's sister. Though he was young when she passed, he held fond memories of her for quite some time, remembering his summer bicycle rides to her home a few blocks away. He would ride in the child seat on the back of his dad's bicycle to visit her almost weekly. When he began to inquire about visiting her after her passing, we did our best to explain about death to him. We talked about the possibility of a place called Heaven existing and some ideas of what it might be like. We discussed the idea that upon passing, our loved-ones may reconnect with their departed loved-ones. Soon after, Benjamin began saying. "Tante Annie went to Heaven's House." It was about a year and a half after her death that I had the dream I call Heaven's House.

In 2001 I attended a dream circle and shared the dream with a woman I did not know. She had approached me to do a dream exercise together. I described the elements of my dream then she tracked the dream for me. She *went into* my dream, while listening to the monotonous beat of shamanic drumming. Her intent was to go into the dreamscape, observe, and return with any information that she found about the chipped heart in my dream such as, to whom it may belong. After fifteen minutes of drumming and dreaming, she returned to her waking state. She reported her findings to me. She had been able to reach the outdoor courtyard in my dream by flying there with her dream guide, an eagle. Once she alighted onto the courtyard, she observed the group of people a bit and was then approached by a woman with brilliant white hair. The woman, she reported, had a "grandmotherly" feel about her. Without asking the woman anything, she was given a message: "Please tell Kellie thank you for remembering me, I appreciate it very much." I was told the woman had an accent.

I was instantly reminded of Tante Annie. Not only, at the age of seventy-eight did she, have striking white hair, but she also spoke with an Austrian accent, an accent she brought with her here to America from her homeland of Austria following World War II.

What I had never told anyone was at the time of her entrance to the hospital for a severe stroke in which she had entered into a coma, I had sat very still for several minutes on my living room sofa, and concentrated on sending Tante Annie prayers and love. I also *let her know* that I would be open to any messages she might want to send. Her stroke had been a particularly traumatic event for my husband Steve who had found her on that evening and had called the ambulance. He had stayed with her in her home and drove immediately to be at the hospital with her as well. He had been very close to his aunt, often visiting to share a meal or help with a house project of some sort. It was Tante Annie's birthday and we had been invited to dinner on the day she had the stroke. We went to her home early at the request of Steve's mom who lived out of town and had been trying to call her all day but could not make contact.

I prayed a lot for her in the brief time she was in the hospital and in the days and months that followed her passing. It was very hard on Steve and his whole family, she was such a wonderful person and a delightful presence at all the family gatherings, she would be—and still is—sorely missed.

When the contents of her well kept and charming home were divided, we received several sentimental pieces that both Steve and I treasure. To this day, I enjoy going through her button collection and have made a few crafts with them for her grand nieces. We remember her often and tell stories about the times we spent with her; they were complete with the embellishments of the phrases she so often used, with her accent to boot, such as she telling us her recipes in which she would add, "just a little bit of butter" (which sounded like "booder.")

Following the dream tracking information I received, I shared the dream and information with my mother-in-law,

Tante Annie's youngest sister. Mom is a big dreamer and often dreams of her departed loved-ones. She is open to the possibility of communicating with departed loved through dreams. She was touched and comforted by Tante Annie's message to me. A few weeks later, on Easter, I placed a crystal heart upon Tante's grave.

Since dreaming of the chipped heart, I have heard many stories that contain elements that suggest one may need to recover a piece of a broken heart. I have made it a practice to deliver crystal hearts to those who *have a story*. This includes my sister Colleen, when Maude, a beloved family cat died and she buried her, and a grieving mother who lost her ten year old son to a horrendous disease and who managed to be an inspiration in the midst of her pain to other mothers. The jade heart I gave to Connie when she entered *the Foundation for Shamanic Studies Three-Year Program* sat on her dream altar for quite some time. Then it managed to find a new home in the hands of one of our workshop attendees, our friend Claudia, who was recovering from cancer and searching for true healing.

Have I found the true recipient of the chipped heart? I am uncertain. When I do ponder my dream I often wonder if I need to return the heart to myself. I'm sure I do. From this dream I have learned two significant things: listen to people's stories with care and we really can meet together in the courtyard of God's house, if only in our dreams.

Chapter 12
Shape Shifting Ancestors: A Mahican Encounter
By Connie Caldes

*Any transition serious enough to alter your definition of self
will require not just small adjustments in your way of living
and thinking but a full-on metamorphosis.*
— Martha Beck

I had an intriguing and powerful dream where I experienced
shape shifting. This dream came quite some time after I
attended my first advanced shamanic workshop in Santa Fe:

Cat People

*I am at a workshop out west, possibly in New Mexico,
possibly in Colorado. We are learning about shamanism, with
Sandra Ingerman. I am staying in a suite of four bedrooms
surrounding a living area. I walk up to my suite and as I enter
the living area, I notice that I am growling. Then, I begin to
transform into a large cat and hiss and growl with great
vigor. I am concerned about what is happening to me. I notice
that my son is sleeping on a bed in the living area. I am
certain that I will not harm him, but I am having the instinct
to leap and bite someone else in the neck. I leap on the bed,
guarding my son as a man enters the room. I sense that my
cat energy is receding and I am relieved. The man comforts
me, telling me that I am only partly cat and that I am shifting
back to human form. He says that people that go to shamanic
workshops eventually experience these transformations. He
says that this will happen to many people spontaneously.*

*Then, he starts to shift into a cat. I decide to take my son
and go in a bedroom and lock the door, remembering my
instincts while a cat. I hide in a bedroom with two people (a
couple) that help put David on a bed in a loft. When I emerge,*

95

the woman across the hall calls me to her room, telling me that she shares a room with the couple's infant. I watch him (the infant) transform into the head of a pre-historic bird. I look into the slow moving eyes of this being and sense that it is on the brink of having a human, feeling conscience. Then I fly up through the clouds and dive down through a storm. As I am struck by lightning, I begin to transform into the cat. I land on the ground and slink around, hoping that no one will notice.

This dream was a doozer, possibly the wildest dream that I recall. I was very thrilled with the sensations of transforming and being the large cat. I really know what it is like to turn into a werewolf!

At a later time, I felt compelled to look through my keepsakes for a WWI medal that had belonged to my grandfather, the same grandfather that provided guidance in earlier dreams, sensing that the large cat might be associated with him. I was amazed to find that my grandfather's 81st Division Medal was coined the *WILDCATS*.

Another dream that including shape shifting came shortly thereafter, at a time when I was having many out of body experiences and also finding that many of my conscious shamanic journeys led me to Native Americans:

The Dream Within a Dream Within a Dream

I am dreaming of sleeping in my bed in my childhood home and dreaming. In that dream, I am looking out a window and a car comes around a bend. I know that the woman in the car is going to crash and die. I feel related to her. The car crashes and I experience her Near Death Experience. I'm exhilarated as I move through tunnels towards beacons of light. Then, I realize that I'm vibrating and that I can lift out of my body. So, I do. I hit the ceiling in my

*childhood home and fly through the wall above the window. I
fly up and down the street that I grew up on with ease and
enjoy every moment of it. Then, I go back to the house and
speak to my mother. An unknown older woman preempts the
conversation and takes me down the hall to stand in front of a
mirror. I try to transform into a Heron and am not successful.
But then, I look at my face. I am eight to ten years younger.
My dream eyes are a cross between my waking eyes and those
of a Native American woman. All I can think is "Who is that?"
I walk down the hall and wake up.*

I have always heard that you should pay attention when
you experience a dream within a dream. It signals multiple
levels of consciousness in action and powerful energy can come
through. And this dream not only had that feature, but also
included an attempt to shape shift. Again, I had a sense of great
energies at work.

I remained perplexed about this dream for a couple of
months, and then attended a lecture at a local public library
given by a Mahican man, Steve. On the way to the talk, a hawk
swooped down over my windshield while I was on a bridge that
crossed the Hudson River, the river that supported life for the
Mahicans.

Steve was very interesting as he described his work to
recover the lost secrets, customs and beliefs of his people who
had been mostly wiped out, with the few left moved from
upstate New York, to Stockbridge, MA and eventually to
Wisconsin. He took great interest in my thoughts and we had a
powerful conversation before the lecture. I could see that he
enjoyed my interest in his work. I cannot help but wonder if our
paths will cross again.

Shortly after attending the lecture, while reading Olga
Kharitidi's *Entering the Circle,* I came across the word *magus.*

I wanted to know more about the definition of this word and the people that might be labeled with it. So, I took out my large dictionary, with three columns on each page and began my search. I found *magus* in the center column of the page, only to have my eyes catch something that magnified in my face in the right column, *Mahican*. But Mahican was not just Mahican. It was in syllable form, therefore it read, *Mah-i-can*. This is what spoke to my soul. In all of my years of seeing that word, I had never realized that *Mah-i-can* was my current married name in reverse. My name, at the time, was Connie Mah, pronounced, *can-i-Mah*. I just knew that the woman in the mirror was part of me and that some great part of me was connected to the Mahicans. And, I should not be surprised since I incarnated close to the Hudson River, the place where my Greek grandfather made his home after emigrating from Greece at age fourteen. And, no wonder I have felt so compelled to make a turtle rattle, one of the Mahican's most powerful totems.

A couple of years ago, just one year after my husband and I separated and I was well on my way to divorce, I met a man, Tom, online. For unexplained reasons, he was the only person that interested me on this dating website. A few days into our cyber conversation, Tom announced, "My great grandmother was 100% Mohican and my favorite movie is *Last of the Mohicans*." We have since watched the film together and I agree – the best movie that I have seen. The best music too! Tom has taken a liking to shamanism and is guided by the Wolf and a Mohican Warrior. He also encounters Turkey and Turtle on a regular basis, the other two Mohican Clan Totems. His spirit teacher, the warrior, has told him that he and I are both Mohican. Why am I surprised?

Frog Memory
By Connie Caldes

It wasn't a creek,
But rather a crick,
A place to explore and wonder.

The frogs were my friends,
My surrogate siblings,
I sat with them for hours.

Their eyes peering up,
Through the glassy surface,
As if to say,
"Come find me."

"At least someone wanted to play!"

So, I sat and watched,
As he challenged my speed,
"Come get me before I submerge."

I lifted my hand,
And reached for his body,
"DARN! I missed him."

But, I didn't give up,
I wanted a connection,
"The next time I won't be fooled."

I engaged my eyes,
Watched with intent,
As I reached to touch my friend.

As he leapt from the side,
I leapt with him,

To the underworld of the crick.

Into the water,
Into the mud,
Covered in the elements.

I emerged with the frog in hand,
Then gently released him.

Chapter 13
Animal Spirit Dreams: The Chocolate Mare
By Kellie Meisl

*A horse is the projection of peoples' dreams about themselves -
strong, powerful, beautiful — and it has the capability of
giving us escape from our mundane existence.*
— Pam Brown

*The essence of a chocolate brown mare with a black mane is
blown into my heart and my crown. I am told that the horse
retrieved for me was in a large field surrounded by a corral.
Other horses were nearby but she is that horse that chose to
come to me. She has much vitality. I am pleased with this
vision; I feel the strength of the Chocolate Mare. I dance to
honor my new Animal Spirit.*

I had this experience at a workshop I attended hosted by
Sandra Ingerman, education director for *The Foundation for
Shamanic Studies.* We each journeyed to the beat of the
shaman's drum to find a power animal for one another. I hadn't
had many experiences with horses and felt surprised and
honored that one would show up for me.

On my way home that day, my mind wandered and I found
myself taking a wrong turn. I describe the event in my dream
journal:

*I think I am at the end of Route 41, turning onto Route 20,
when actually I am only at the end of Route 295. I've taken my
right turn too soon. An inner voice tells me that this is not
accidental; I have taken the wrong turn for a reason. I decide
to go on a little further. I ask for a sign to show me if there is a
purpose for me to travel this way. I immediately spot a
blinking yellow light on this rural route. I get the message—
slow down. As I do so, I look to my right and see a large hill*

sloping downward; it is a dirt road. I know I should go down this road but doubt myself.

I continue on to the center of the small town I am in. I see nothing significant and realize I must return to the dirt road.

As I go down the hill, I pass two walkers who do not seem to notice me. I continue for about a half-mile. The land is heavily wooded and only dotted with a few homes. At the end of the road I come to a clearing on my right. On a hill I see a red barn, with a field around it and a corral surrounding the field. As I begin to turn my car around in the barn's driveway, I look up on the hill and see a tall chocolate brown horse with a black mane staring down at me. The horse continues to look at me and I feel the need to walk to the horse, an act I would not normally take with a strange animal on private land.

I walk up the long driveway and reach the horse. It is taller than any animal I have ever stood inches from; it towers over me. I want to touch it but I feel scared. I decide to reach my hand out with the intention that if the horse moves toward me, I will touch its nose. It comes forth and with held breath I touch its nose gently. We stare at each other for a few moments. Then, the horse slowly turns to its right, facing west, the direction in which I attended the workshop. I slowly return to my car. The horse never moves again and remains facing to the west as I leave. On my way back up the dirt hill a message, audible in my mind comes to me, "You are on the right path..."

Power animals, as they are called in the language of shamans and healers, can come in many forms. In shamanic practices one can retrieve a power animal for oneself, or, as in my workshop experience, one can be retrieved for another person. Often, we ask for power animals to reveal themselves to us during a shamanic journey and to become our guides in the Spirit World. These animals can take us to other worlds and lead us toward information we can use to heal the mind, body or spirit of our self or others. Michael Harner, founder of *The Foundation for Shamanic Studies* and author of *The Way of the Shaman*, teaches us in his work that we can ask our power animal to journey to an ill person who is in need of support in order assist the healing process.[12] It is understood that healing takes place on a level intended for each individual and comes forth through the Spirit World, not by means of the person who is journeying. Power animals therefore, can act as conduits for those who are in need of healing some aspect of their life.

Though I have worked with power animals in the ways aforementioned, I also work with real power animals that exist in my everyday life. This practice came to me even before I began reading about shamanic practices and attending workshops relating to this field. But, then again, shamanic practices seem to enter into ones life in a seemingly fortuitous way. At least that has been my experience.

Power animals came into my life around the time I began my meditative walking practices and started studying dreams. One day, after a particularly healing journey of intense meditative walking, I felt I received clarity about my life's purpose. I asked for a sign to confirm this. I knew immediately to turn on to a dirt path that would take me to the winding brook that runs along the backyards of my home and my neighbors. When I reached the brook, there stood Great Blue Heron; I received my sign. We stared at each other for a few moments, then it took to flight, its massive wings undulating rhythmically as it rose. The message was clear: my dreams were taking flight. To me, Great Blue Herons also speak of moving through the waters of life slowly, making sure to take each step

---

[12] Michael Harner, *The Way of the Shaman* (New York: HarperCollins, 1990) p. 102.

with intention and persevering during periods of crisis—or even life's doldrums. This is an important message for me to heed. Ted Andrews, in *Animal Speak*, expresses Great Blue Heron as signifying "aggressive self-determination."[13] I also believe this to be true.

The first time I laid eyes on a Red-Tailed Hawk was when I was walking with my son Benjamin when he was three, in a local wildlife refuge. We were joined by a couple of our neighborhood friends. As we approached our cars to leave, the hawk alighted on the sign that stands at the entrance (and exit) of the path into the park. We were no more than six feet away from it. I could look into its yellow eyes. It was an awesome experience that led me to begin working with Hawk, known to some as a messenger of the Spirit World. Soon after, I spotted Hawk again nearby the refuge in a tree at a neighboring yard. Then, not too long after that, I asked Hawk to appear for a third time as gesture that I should heed the advice of a dream I had. As I drove by the same area again, Hawk sat up on the telephone wires above the entrance to the wildlife preserve. The need to follow the advice of my dream was further affirmed by the fact that the bird sat on communication wires.

These are a few dramatic examples of how I have worked with *animal energy*. I notice animals appear with messages almost daily in my life when I pay attention.

Soon after my father-in-law's passing, a red capped male house finch, one of the few I'd seen that winter, alighted on my deck during morning coffee to taunt me. A little joke from Steve's Dad no doubt; he and I carried on the disagreement forever about whether the little reddish birds that landed at his feeder were male house finches as I believed them to be, or

---

[13] Ted Andrews, *Animal Speak* (St. Paul: Llewellyn Publications, 1993) p. 156.

purple finches, as he believed they were. We always got a good laugh, agreeing to disagree about that bird.

Just as purple finch reminds me of my father-in-law, so does goldfinch remind me of my own father. When I was a child, my father used to recite a silly poem about a little yellow bird. I would beg him to recite the poem over and over. When he passed, I placed the sweet little poem into his casket, sending it along with him as a sign that the little yellow bird would forever link us. He passed in the spring; I am sure when the little yellow birds return to me in each spring, they carry with them a little of his spirit.

Birds have a particularly spiritual connotation for me as they have the ability to take flight to the heavens and yet they alight here on earth. For me they signify a bridge between heaven and earth; a bridge in flight if you will.

Deer, an animal that is very earth-based in its lifestyle, reaches toward the heavens with its antlers. When we had just learned of my son's conception, my husband and I found a pair of matching antlers, seemingly left there for us, in the backyard of his parent's home. We had gone there, in the dustings of December's snow, to check the property, as his Dad lay very ill in a hospital bed. He was not expected to return home but soon after he made a miraculous recovery. Were the deer antlers a sign of new life—both for my son and my father-in-law?

Five years later, when his health again took a turn for the worse, three deer appeared to him regularly in the weeks before his death. They would come up on the deck right in front of the large glass doors of his daughter Nancy's condominium in the suburbs to feed right before him as he lay a few feet away. He was amazed to see that one was a thriving fawn. It was surviving in the cold of winter, against all odds. Deer, he noted, never gave birth in the freezing winter months for their young could not survive the harsh weather conditions. It made him laugh to think these three city deer would appear to him so boldly. He had never seen the likes of it on the wooded acres of his own home in the thirty years he had lived there, he would tell us. Steve's dad passed on a cold January day soon after seeing the baby deer. His ninth grandchild, baby Liberty, met him on the way no doubt, for she was born during the hours of his passing.

When beginning shamanic work, I was assigned the task of receiving a personal power animal that I would work with. I was taking a class with Sandra Ingerman at the Omega Institute at the time. The animal that appeared to me in the journey I went on to the beat of the shaman's drum was rabbit. Since I had so many spontaneous encounters with animals in the wild, I placed an intention that I would receive confirmation in everyday life that rabbit was indeed the animal I was to work with when doing shamanic healing journeys. Sure enough, on my second day of the training, on my drive to Omega, a rabbit crossed my path and slipped into a patch of bushes, a *portal* I use to this day when journeying.

For those who wish to work with power animals in their own life, I say simply: pay attention to the amazing wildlife not only in your dreams but in your everyday life as well—they have messages for you.

Wildfire
By Kellie Meisl

Masculine aspect of the feminine mare
Who had just been retrieved for me,
Chocolate, how apropos,
My addiction,
Sweet.

So huge he scared me
I stood in paused breath,
"Can I touch you?"
My request is granted.

I extend myself slowly,
It's such a brief moment in forever,
He turns to the west...

My inner voice whispers,
"You are on the right path."

Chapter 14
Sanibel Dreaming: Fusing with the Elements
By Connie Caldes

I am sunlight, slicing the dark. Who made this night?
— Rumi

For me, Sanibel Island is a safe place. Many healing visions have come from her waters, the resident dolphins and manatees, not to mention the alligators. My daughter and I love to shell together and do so each spring. Our favorites include the Shark Eye, the Lightning Welk, the Sea Urchin, the tiny Wentle Trap and the beloved Baby's Ear. Beneath a table in our living room, we have placed a large Italian glass jar full of our most precious shells. A small jar upon the same table houses our Baby's Ears and another holds our Wentle Traps. However, one precious Sanibel shell is missing in our home, the Junonia.

Shortly after hurricane Charley, which ravaged Sanibel in August of 2004, I dream:

Finding a Junonia

I am wading in Sanibel's gulf waters, looking for shells. To my left, I notice a cat-walk-like cement structure along the water's edge. Resting on the edge of this structure, I find a beautiful shell. I quickly realize that I have found a Junonia. I show friends and family my prize shell, commenting that on Sanibel, you get your picture in the paper for this discovery. I look on the "bottom" of the shell and notice something that resembles the heel of a woman's shoe. I am most intrigued with the heel.

Then I walk along the coast, looking into tidal pools, noticing beautiful bright colored fish. I leave the beach and walk near the reception desk of my hotel. I see mourning doves on fence. One of the doves, a male, joyfully jumps onto my finger and speaks to me in English. Distracted with my new friend, I miss my ride to dinner with my family.

Junonia is named for the Goddess Juno, protectress of the well being of women. What a lovely symbol to dream. I felt that I had received the gift of protection from the Goddesses. And, protection had come to the beautiful island of Sanibel in my dream, much needed in the wake of hurricane Charley, with hurricanes Frances and Ivan on their way.

I spoke of my Junonia dream with Kellie who promptly said that for her "heel" was a metaphor for "heal." This also felt wonderful, especially since the "heel" was on the "sole" or "soul" of the Junonia shoe.

So, what do I make of the Junonia shell in my dream? Was she a gift from Juno? Was she healing for my soul? Surely all things were pointing to her femininity. Would she bring protection for Sanibel during future hurricanes? These questions remain unanswered, part of the mystery of the dream. But I am quite certain that the multi-faceted gifts of this dream will continue to reveal themselves to me for years to come.

The work with the Junonia dream brought me back to waking dreams on Sanibel. In one case, I was walking at dusk on a sandbar with my family. Something no larger than one inch square caught my eye in the sand. So I dug and dug and dug to unearth a live Lightning Welk, about a foot long! It was a breath-taking animal. I had never seen such a large and beautiful snail, complete with pink, cream and brown markings. I took it out far beyond the sandbar and released it where it would not be disturbed or illegally taken by a greedy *sheller.*

The following year, I had a similar experience while walking with a *sheller* of twenty years named Michael, a principal in an LA middle school. A small glint caught my eye on the sandbar. I dug out a large and perfect Shark Eye. Usually, the Shark Eye snail is killed by an Auger as evidenced by the hole left in the side of the empty Shark Eye shell. In this case, no Auger hole, only sheer perfection. And it was huge for a Shark Eye. Michael commented immediately, "in my twenty years of shellin', I have never found one that good." Later, Michael's mother told me that Michael "wanted to pop my head off." I had found a winner with no animal inside, a prize to take home and cherish. Was this a reward for throwing back the Lightning Welk?

My Junonia dream also brings to mind a sleeping dream that I had on Sanibel, in May of 2000. I had noticed that year that my dreams on Sanibel were more ethereal, with vivid colors, leaving me with a feeling of contact with the upper worlds.

Goddess Messenger

I am looking at a newspaper article and notice a photo to the left. The image in the photo becomes alive. The image includes my husband and me in an embrace, sitting on a rock in a waterfall, surrounded by greenery. Above us stands a TALL and slender, pixie-like, winged Goddess. Her hands are together, in prayer position, over her head and pointing to the heavens. I am stunned by the image!

I always felt that this dream came to show me that my relationship with my husband was sacred and guarded by divine forces, even though marriage ended in a divorce.

Later, when doing some further work with this image, my psyche cried out: *She's not a Goddess; she's a Fairy!* It seems that I have neglected my Irish roots and need to do further work here. I should have known that fairies can be huge, not just the tiny variety that stereotypically flit about the flowers. And, certainly, the wings should have been a big hint as to her heritage amongst the devas.

I have taken shamanic journeys to this deva in the time since I first dreamed of her. In one case, she performed an upper world healing on a friend. In another journey, she fed me an apple. This is the only time that I have eaten in a journey and I am sure that transformational gifts came from eating her *non-forbidden* fruit. I have a sense that my relationship with her will grow clearer in the future, now that I have acknowledged her true nature.

Another Sanibel dream with vivid color occurred in early 2001, after going through a period of time when I felt constant angst regarding a relationship with a woman. I had known her for many years, and she seemed controlling and judgmental to me whenever we were together.

At some point I realized that my discomfort with her behavior was only going to hurt me, and I began to pray for the grace to forgive her for not honoring our long relationship. It had become clear that she was not going to change.

I prayed for the grace to forgive before the Sanibel waves, and within a few nights, I had a spectacular visual dream:

Magical Midnight Sky

I am at a high school reunion. I look up to see a glorious midnight blue sky, sparking with stars. I notice people dancing throughout the sky. Then, while pointing upward and to the left, I say, "look at that!" A beautiful swan in descending flight emerges from the heavens.

When I woke, I knew that I had received a gift, yet I did not have a fix on its nature. Usually, I do not use dream dictionaries, but in this case, I decided to look up *Swan* in Jamie Sams' *Medicine Cards*. There on the page lay the word *swan*, below it the Native American symbolic meaning, *grace*.[14] Ask and you shall receive! And, I can't help but wonder what will occur at my high school reunion later this year!

So, Sanibel brings me physical and spiritual gifts from the higher worlds, including the elemental and deva realms. I have a sense that this makes certain that Sanibel is a special place on our planet, a place where we get in touch with nature, the ocean, the sea animals, earth, wind, sun and the beings *reflected* in celestial world, be they Goddess, Fairy or Bird, that return us to our own divinity.

---

[14] Jamie Sams, *Medicine Cards* (New York: St. Martin's Press, 1988) p. 193.

Chapter 15
Lucid Dreaming: Bedside Visitors
By Kellie Meisl

They tease me now, telling me it was only a dream. But does it matter whether it was a dream or reality, if the dream made known to me the truth.
— Fyodor Dostoyevsky

I make an intention before I go to sleep; I write it on a slip of paper and place it under my pillow: *I ask for a power animal to be in my dreams tonight.*

Tiger's Eyes

I am flying around in my dream, sending light to loved-ones, my new dream practice. I send light to Steve and my sister, Colleen as they sit, chatting in my family room (as they had done in waking reality nine days prior). I try to send light to my physical body as it lies in my bed below me. But, as I look down I cannot see my body, only the white sheets and my son Benjamin who lies sleeping beside me. Soon I return to the place in my bed where my physical body is sleeping. Upon re-entering my body, I see a medium-sized tiger; its yellow green eyes lit up, staring at me. Perhaps the message of the tiger is one of light. Perhaps his eyes were telling me I too can see in the dark, the darkness of my dreams.

Bedside visitors, as I like to call them, have appeared frequently in my dreams. These dreams are set apart from other dreams I have. They are lucid in nature and often play out in physically real settings with small hints of alteration such as a moved piece of furniture or an open window to let me know I am dreaming. They have casts of characters who differ from the usual dream players as well. By this, I mean I communicate with them in a more *direct* manner than I would normally.

Sometimes bedside visitors come because they are summoned, as in the case of the tiger where I had asked for guidance. Other times, they come spontaneously. Some bear messages and some appear lost. Whatever the case, they continue to come when I'm cordial to receiving them.

I once awoke to see a man standing on the opposite side of my bed. He had long, wavy, brown hair and a full beard. I asked him if he was my guide and he told me he was. When I asked him if he had a message for me he said, "You write the story and I'll provide the illustrations." I took this message to be literal at the time since I wanted to write a picture book for children. I went ahead and wrote a story, then waited a little while to see if an illustrator would show up. Later, chatting at a bookstore with another woman in line, she mentioned her son was in college and wanted to become a picture book illustrator. I felt sure this was the serendipitous moment so I gave her my card. But, it never panned out. Finally, I gave up and illustrated it myself with collage and painting. Maybe the man was trying to tell me he would provide the inspirations for my pictures. Another interpretation of this message may be that I am in charge of creating the story of my life. As I rewrite this story for this book I am creating, I feel that I am writing the words the visitor referred to. I feel his presence with me whenever I write.

That dream reminds me of a similar bedside visitor who came thirty-five years earlier, when I was four. He too had long brown hair and a beard. I felt frightened by this unknown visitor. Then, one night after he visited I went downstairs to my father to tell him of my scary dream. He listened patiently then said, "Maybe he is a good man, a friend. Maybe there is a reason he came to you." That's all I needed to hear. I came to believe he was watching over me as a friend. Now I wonder: Were both men in my dreams the same man? And, I am reminded of the gift my father gave me; he taught me to heed the messages of my dreams.

One night a person in a pink iridescent space suit entered through the wall at the foot of my bed. When I asked the visitor who it was, I heard, "I'm from the United States Space Program." Suspicious, for reasons that hold no logic, I cast it out of my room. It left through the tiny crack of the window between the sash and sill, shedding its pink skin and leaving it behind. I think that was a lost visitor.

Probably the most profound visitor I've had to date was a being I originally named *The Moon Goddess*:

In this dream I am out and about, flying in my room and trying to penetrate the wall to the outside, which I can do to no avail. Finally, I decide to return to bed. As I do so, I fly low to the floor and come upon a pure, white, shroud-like material hovering slightly above the floor, beside my bed. There are layers and layers of the sheer white material making it opaque. As my eyes moved upward, I see that it is the gown of a being. Still moving upward I meet her face; it too is pure white, with effulgent blue eyes and blood red lips. Above her head are thousands of suspended pearls that seem to form a tall crown. How these pearls stay in place I cannot see? I asked her if she is my Guardian Angel and she laughs and says, "Yes." I get the feeling she is saying, "Yes, if that's what you need me to be." Then I ask her if she has a message for me. She begins to fade away; I can only make out the words, "Remember Dr. Del...." I struggled to hear more but she is gone. (To this day, I wonder when this information will come in handy.)

Sometimes I imagine her to be my deceased grandmother, Nanny who I lost at age five. She too had radiant blue eyes. In fact, she loved all shades of blue. Funny, since this dream I can't get enough of the color blue either. Other times I imagine my bedside visitor to be the Blessed Mother Mary. Either way she is a Mother to me and she has brought me a renewed faith not only in life but also in the strong possibility of another kind of life existing after death. This is a theme that recurs over and over in my dreams.

I recently made a dream mask in my shamanic women's group to honor the Mother/Goddess/Guardian of my dream. The mask is a plaster casting of my own face. She is pure white; her blue eyes are my blue eyes when I wear the mask. She has blood red lips. She wears a pearl crown and has a moonstone on her third eye. She now hangs nearby to the original location of where she revealed herself. At night I look at her often as I lie in bed. I have come to realize that in many ways she *is* an aspect of me. I too have blue eyes. Her whiteness represents my purest form, and the white of my skin. I have to wonder if that is why she laughed when I asked her if she was my Guardian Angel. Sometimes I think now that she is telling me she *is* my Guardian, a Goddess, my Mother, and a higher aspect of myself. Her simple, "Yes" somehow revealed the multi-layered aspects of the soul to me and the *whole* of who I really am...

Chapter 16
Community and Healing: A Shamanic Dream Ritual
By Connie Caldes

And say my glory was I had such friends.
— William Butler Yeats

When I completed my seven weeks of radiation, I decided to invite friends to come over and participate in a ritual where I would put closure on my experience and say good-bye to breast cancer. Seven women arrived on that beautiful evening in July. We sat around a beautiful altar, decorated with sacred objects brought by all participants.

A Poem for Sue
By Connie Caldes

Sue, my surrogate mom
Creator of art
Storehouse of myth and secret
My friend
My tea sister
Baker of white CHOCOLATE
She loves the feminine instinct
Our bodies
Our breasts
Supporter of all women
On their paths
To self-discovery
She was there
There with me
On that awful day
The day that the doctor said
"You have breast cancer"

I saw the tear
Flow down her cheek
When he told me
But she wiped it away
And sat with me
And told me
"I have several friends who have had this"
"And, they all have beat it"
It was important to hear that
While I could only think of death
It sank in
And I remember
Yes, I remember the comfort
Of having a friend
At my side
On that dreadful day

The ceremony began with honoring the four directions, led by Sue. Then, Kira burned sage and performed a shamanic cleansing on me, with special emphasis on releasing attachments that had been unhealthy and part of my lesson in surviving cancer. After the cleansing, participants shared whatever they wished about healing and love. Kellie wrote a piece that she read during the ceremony, a powerful story that was grown from many of my dreams. I closed the ceremony by sounding a delicate chime over the head of my friends and telling them about how special they were to me. We ended with a beautiful song, *Amazing Grace*, a version that was intertwined with the song of whales.[15]

I felt relieved and healed by this ritual, cleansed of all of the turmoil that had ensued in the prior months. I was done with treatment. What a relief! And, although I was ready to

---

[15] Cecilia, *Voice of the Femine Spirit* [CD]. 1999.

move on, I found that I remained quite vulnerable. I felt depressed and unable to emerge from my home and cocoon of safety, a bit unable to socialize and interact in the larger world.

I recall the turning point. I was in Maine on vacation, depressed and not talking to people. A friendly couple that I met the year prior came to the picnic table where I sat looking demoralized and said, "Are you OK?" I answered swiftly and honestly, "No, I just completed treatment for breast cancer and I am depressed." They were both very loving and understanding. That conversation began another process of healing for me. I was down a bit for the two months that followed, but it was generally uphill from that point on. By Christmas, I started to *forget* about the cancer. Life seemed normal again.

Strange as it seems, I was more tired after I felt better. It seemed that I was more in touch with what I really needed, and part of what I needed was long periods of sleep. So that winter, I slept a lot. I would wake up in the later part of the morning with powerful and vivid dreams. Then, I would often go out for tea with a friend. For as long as I did this, I felt a sense of bodily healing coming from the sleep and dreams. I didn't need to analyze anything. I just needed to sleep and connect with my community.

Healing requires community, those that understand, validate, check-in and spend time with us. I needed to know that people were there and that they would sit with me, laugh with me and allow me to cry when necessary. Fortunately, I have many such friends. Some feel blessed to have never endured what I did. Others have been through much worse. It is a spectrum of challenges that we all face, and each of us must find those who reside on various levels of this continuum to support us in our healing.

Some people run in the other direction and want no part of knowing who you are in your crisis, but I suspect that these individuals did not get support during some trauma in their life, left the issues unresolved and consequently have no capacity to provide meaningful support. Ironically, some of these people refer to themselves as healers, an unfortunate misnomer.

As my community came together for me and I got beyond the cancer, I had the following dream:

Art in a Bottle

I am back at Tufts University, my alma mater. I am in engineering school but much more interested in an art contest. I decide to enter the contest even though creating my piece will cause me to miss my math class. I am in a large room with many people working on their art project. I ask about supplies but realize that I am to use mostly my own personal belongings in this project. I place clear, blue glass stones in the bottom of a straight and narrow clear, glass vase and then add three pictures toward the bottom, facing out. One of the pictures seems related to my son. My project is a bit like flower arranging, only the items arranged are not flowers. The project is to "ask a question" and "answer the question" through its presentation. I want to ask, "Will I be an author?" But, I find that the question doesn't feel right to me. It seems a bit arrogant. So, I ask, "Is writing part of my future?"

The scene shifts to the next day. I am working on my project in the engineering building. My daughter tells me that I missed my Spanish class that seems more like her Latin class. I realize that like my daughter, I am expected to know vocabulary in another language. The glass vase is now a huge bottle, about six feet tall and four feet wide, with a narrow top. I now have many things in my bottled art project. I place groupings of stones on the bottom in rough rose quartz, smooth Turquoise River stones and smooth blue lapis lazuli. One of the lapis lazuli stones is about one half inch thick and perfectly round. I have two large stuffed animals facing out in the back of the bottle display, one bright blue, and the other bright red. I place feathers coming out the top of the bottle: bald eagle, owl, hawk, turkey and an unknown white feather. I don't know where to place the question but figure out that I need to write it on a strip of white paper and tape it to the outside of the bottle. I place a miniature ironing board in a clearing amongst the stones at the bottom of the bottle. I place a small open book on the ironing board. The left page reads, "Casting the Heroine," the right side "by Connie Caldes." I understand that I am creating my own questions and answers in this lifetime.

At the last minute, I go to a library that has my dream room altar in the center of the floor. I grab my lavender beaded silk shawl from the altar and place it on the stones inside of the bottle.

I received many messages from this dream. I felt that I was instructed to express my creativity in a community of learners. The dream showed me that it was OK to choose artistic over analytical endeavors. I created many new crafts and have been much more active in my writing since having this dream.

Not too long ago, I had another powerful dream about healing, but this time it seemed to be telling me that it was my turn to give back to community.

Godly Voice in the Rustic Cathedral

I am at a retreat center in the Adirondacks. I will be attending a workshop with Sandra Ingerman.

The scene shifts and I am still at the retreat center. I am with a Russian man, about 35 years old. He is a soul mate and I feel very close to him. He is grieving over the loss of his two-year-old son, and I feel very sad for him.

The scene shifts again and I am waking from a nap and walking into a rustic cathedral at the same retreat center. Sandra Ingerman sits near the altar. A voice comes from overhead and says, "You have a wish!" I make a remark in return and the source of the voice misinterprets my intention and says, "Do you want three wishes?" I reply, "No, I want one wish." At this point I request that the Russian man be re-united with his lost two-year-old son and my wish is granted. I see the Russian man with a two-year-old boy in the front right corner of the room. There is joy as they are re-united.

At this point, Sandra Ingerman approaches and says, "Connie, it is very powerful that you did not get caught up in fear about your cancer and ask for a guarantee that you would never get cancer again. Rather, you did something for somebody else."

Later, I take the Russian man and his son to the airport. They are going home. I am sad to say good-bye.

I was powerfully affected by this dream that put some closure on several previous nightmares. The dream suggested to me that I was reclaiming part of my masculine side, a part that I needed to heal in order to give back to community. The dream let me know that I had moved beyond fear and that I was ready to assist others. What a blessing!

Part of honoring this dream and new phase in my life came about a year later when I was invited to help plan and execute a community event called *Think Pink*. I was contacted by a local organization, The Storefront Artist Project, and asked if I would like to participate by displaying the breast casts creating in my *Casting the Heroine* workshop. I was thrilled!

As it turned out, over thirty artists donated their work in order to start a scholarship fund for women with breast cancer who wished to participate in art workshops as part of their healing. I was told that the *Casting the Heroine* workshop would qualify for scholarships.

The actual *Think Pink* event was exhilarating. Hundreds of people came out that Friday evening, dressed in pink, to see the art exhibit.

Additional attractions at the gathering included pink treats that resembled breasts and *boobie* prizes. The crowd was sizzling. Survivors were gleeful. It was, by far the most fun cancer event I ever attended. And yes, we were going to do it again next year. Who would have ever thought that breast cancer could be such a source of joy and creativity on the part of a community? We have now completed five annual *Think Pinks* in five consecutive years.

For the 2nd Annual *Think Pink*, I created a turtle rattle, as instructed by my Mohican Grandmother spirit teacher, to honor survivors. Each time I create a rattle, I feel that I heal a part of myself, and hopefully, part of the world.

After the 4th Annual *Think Pink*, the *Think Pink* team was given the opportunity to create a sacred sand mandala with Tibetan Monks during a week at The Colonial Theatre (a national restoration site) in Pittsfield, MA. The monks taught breast cancer survivors and families the art of sand mandala creation and the meaning behind the art: that life and beauty are impermanent and that all prayers return to the oceans of our world. Such was the case when the monks destroyed their own mandala along with the *Think Pink* Mandala and returned the sacred sand to the local Housatonic River so that all of the prayers and healing energy in the mandalas could travel down the river and into the ocean to heal the entire world.

Now I sit here five years later, with the 5th Annual *Think Pink* Art Exhibit just completed at The Colonial Theatre. Over fifty artists participated. Hundreds of people enjoyed the reception and art. The exhibit sprang from the seed of breast casts, iterated through five renditions, interacted with Tibetan Monks, and now comes to a new fruition.

Dreaming in Community with Saddam*
By Connie Caldes

I dreamed of Iraq
a marble palace
searching for Saddam
with PEACEFUL intention

I asked him to join me
in dream circle with others
a union of FRIENDS
a place to be safe

I looked to the sky
concerned about air raids
and silently knew
our SHARING must go on

He dreamed of a hawk
in a circle of Americans
I responded emphatically
"You must let your HEART soar"

He showed me his soft side
and he gave me a gift
I left a better human
for being able to LOVE him

*dreamed in February of 2003, about two months before the
second Iraq War

Chapter 17
Planting Dream Seeds for Connie: Growing the Dream
By Kellie Meisl

Imagination lays the tracks for the Reality Train to drive follow.
— Caroline Casey

In the summer of 2002, Connie asked me to write a story about the descent into darkness she experienced upon the diagnosis of her breast cancer. She wanted me to read the piece at her healing ritual.

I gave myself a week to dream on it. During one of my meditative walks, I realized I wanted to compose a new dream for Connie. This dream would be a compilation of waking and sleeping dreams she had shared with me as well as some new dreams of my own. I envisioned that these new dreams would become little seeds to be planted as Connie accepted them into her own fertile self. I held the intention that they would continue to grow peace, strength and beauty for Connie in her new life, the life that came after the descent into breast cancer, a life of grace.

Growing Wings

In my dream you are riding a white horse. It has a temperamental nature and I am in awe of your courage to take this risk and ride this horse. As I watch you, the horse rears back on its hind legs and kicks its front legs high toward the sky. You are thrown from its back and fall into a place of darkness, the Deep Place. There, by the roots of a tree, Wolf Pine Grandmother is waiting for you. She beckons you to come closer. You walk to her and lean in to her to hear what she has to say. But, instead of speaking, she blows a small seed into your heart. The seed contains knowledge for you and for you to impart onto others. You will begin a journey.

Deer joins you; he will be your companion for the first leg of your journey. Together with deer you go forth into the darkness following the roots of the tree. Each root provides a path for you to take on your quest.

As you go along, some of the paths lead you to people and places that seem familiar. Here you feel supported and loved. As you open your heart and share your truths with these people, the seed inside your heart begins to grow. In turn, they feel safe to share their truths with you. Relationships based on trust, mutual support and love are formed. You notice the roots to these people and places are connected to one another. You recognize these paths; each brings you to friends, guides, teachers and students to whom you can always return.

On other paths you find people and places where you share a truth or two and they with you. But, each sharing is brief and each time you realize you must move on. You notice that the roots, which took you here, are short, not very deep. The seed in your heart continues to grow and blossom.

Other paths lead you to people and places where you share your truths but they are not heard. You open your heart to them but they are incapable of meeting you with their truths. The flower in your heart grows some thorns. You look down and realize the roots to the tree do not grow here.

Then a Great Bear appears to you. He performs a dance for you and he intrigues you. He beckons you to follow him along his path. You are drawn further into the Deep Place. On this path you learn many valuable lessons about yourself, who you really are and your reason for being. You learn to follow *your dreams. You work hard to manifest your life's purpose. At times the path branches and you follow these new roots, finding new teachers. A guide appears and hands you a map. It is the map of your life that you have created while on your journey. You begin to examine it closely. You can see the paths of your truths and you realize these are now the paths you must follow.*

Now, the Bear begins to act suspiciously. He scrambles back to the past roots you have followed with him and tries to claw his way back up the tree. Alarmed, you build safe walls and a roof around yourself; you retreat indoors for safety. He opens your door and comes inside. He has a message for you; in a loud booming voice he shouts a threat at you. He tries to shake your confidence and confuse you. He wants you to walk his path only. In a final act of desperation, the Bear takes his own life, plunging a sharp quill into his own heart. You heed the warning of this Great Bear paying homage to it by molding its likeness in clay with your own hands and finally giving it away.

As you turn to leave, you see a mirror. Looking back at you is your own face. As you stare at yourself, the face of a Native American woman merges with yours and you become one. She smiles at you. There is a deep knowing that you are connected to the true teachers of your past, present and future. You walk on a little further and a chorus of African singers meets you. They greet you singing in beautiful harmony. They sing to you a song of honor, a song of healing, their song acknowledges your courage to grow and move forward from the darkness. They don beautiful ceremonial gowns in a rainbow of iridescent silks. One steps forward. She begins to pull threads from her gown, the strands of silk flash in the bright sunlight, iridescent green, ruby, violet. She opens her hand and presents to you a hummingbird. From her gown a hummingbird has been made. She places it on your heart. It inserts its long pointed beak into your heart, drinking the nectar from the blossoming flower. The petals unfold in magical beauty. The tiny bird goes in still deeper and removes the thorns, which had formed on the flower. You begin to fly.

Now you are flying over the top of your life map reviewing your journey. You see the many faces of those you love and who love you; you realize they have been they with you on your journey all along. You see the places you have gone and some new places you might be going. You see the faces of those you have left behind; they are hollow plastic statues. These people hold no power over you now.

You return to Wolf Pine Grandmother, she is waiting for you. She again blows into your heart. This time your heart opens and a group of baby herons flutter forth, released from deep inside. The white horse is there to meet you, it now has wings, and it is there to bring you home. You climb on it's back and ascend to your present life. In my dream you are sitting in your living room, in a circle of woman who love you. We have come to learn from you, to hear about your journey, to honor your truths.

Planting dream seeds is a wonderful tool for healing. In her award-winning children's book *Tar Beach*, Faith Ringgold, an African American woman who grew up in Harlem in the 1930's, understands the power of planting dream seeds. Cassie Louise Lightfoot, the protagonist in her story, plants seeds for herself by taking dream flight. She soars above places that she and her family are segregated from in waking life and claims them as her own in the dream realm. Because the waking world and dream world are of one continuum, we can surmise that her life is positively affected by this dream. We see this in the pleasant nature of the story and art illustrations, a quilt Ringgold invents, sewing each piece of the story, manifesting it a stitch at a time. Ringgold puts it best in her story when Cassie proclaims: "Me, Cassie Louise Lightfoot, only eight years old and in the third grade and I can fly. That means I am free to go wherever I want for the rest of my life."[16]

---

[16] Faith Ringgold, *Tar Beach* (Albuquerque: Dragonfly Books, 1996) p. 10.

Chapter 18
Honoring a Sojourner: The Good Mother's Dream
By Connie Caldes

When an inner situation is not made conscious, it appears as fate.
— Carl Jung

Many years ago, The Women's Service Center of Western Massachusetts and The Rape Crisis Center of Berkshire County consolidated to create Elizabeth Freeman Center. As a member of the new board, I couldn't help but wonder if we had chosen our new name for mystical reasons that were beyond our current knowing. Since that time, I have read many accounts of Elizabeth Freeman's (Mumbet) life as a slave and her desire for liberty. One does not have to look too deep to find the simple but beautiful gift of her story.

The person who wrote most passionately about Mumbet was Catharine Sedgwick, an accomplished novelist and daughter of Theodore Sedgwick, the attorney that helped Mumbet gain her freedom from slavery in 1781. After winning her freedom, Mumbet helped raise Theodore Sedgwick's children, including Catharine Sedgwick who loved her dearly. She was keenly aware of Mumbet's special and dignified persona. In her *Essay on Mumbet,* Catharine Sedgwick wrote:

"Action was the law of her nature – conscious of superiority to all around her a state of servitude was intolerable. It was not the work, work was play to her. Her power of executive was marvelous. Nor was it awe of her kind master or fear of her despotic mistress. But it was the gulling of the harness, the irrepressible longing for liberty."[17]

---

[17] Mary Wilds, Mumbet: The Life and Times of Elizabeth Freeman (Greensboro: Avisson Press Inc., 1999) p. 63.

Mumbet was born into slavery in Claverack, NY. At some point in her childhood, she was transferred to Sheffield, MA to John Ashley, an attorney and most prominent citizen of his community. She had previously been "owned" by John Ashley's father-in-law, Pieter Hockaboom.

In 1768, John Ashley was among the 17 out of 109 legislators in Massachusetts who did not support Boston's defiance of English rule. But four years later, he had a change of heart. During the winter of 1772-1773, eleven Sheffield men, including John Ashley, met in the second floor study of the Ashley house and wrote the Sheffield Declaration of Independence. Some consider this to be the first formal Declaration of Independence from England. Many meetings regarding independence, the constitution of Massachusetts, and the Bill of Rights ensued in that study in the years that followed.

For many years, Mumbet was privy to these meetings as she served the men food and beverages. As soon as the constitution of Massachusetts became law in 1781, Mumbet demanded her own freedom. She was later asked how she learned about principles of freedom and replied,

"By keepin' still and mindin' things."[18]

When further questioned as to what she "minded", it was explained,

"for instance, when she was waiting at table, she heard gentlemen talking over the Bill of Rights and the new constitution of Massachusetts; and in all they said she never heard but that all people were born free and equal and she

---

[18] Ibid., p. 65.

thought long about it, and resolved she would try whether she did not come in among them."[19]

Some people say that Mumbet filed suit after her mistress struck her with a hot shovel, but Catharine Sedgwick emphasizes that it was the American ideals of freedom that were her inspiration.

I believe that Mumbet had her own powerful dream of liberty and absorbed the dream of the colonists since it was so related to her own. The beauty was that their dream included a solution to her dilemma, a legal basis for liberty. So, she rode on the coattails of their dream and like them, won her freedom, in Berkshire County Court of Common Pleas, Great Barrington, MA.

After being freed, Mumbet said:

"Any time, any time while I was a slave, if one minute's freedom had been offered to me and I had been told I must die at the end of that minute, I would have taken it, just to stand one minute on God's earth a free woman, I would."[20]

It is well known that Mumbet applied the ideals of the colonists' desire for liberty to herself, but it is often stated in a dry and analytical way with little or no attention to the magic in what occurred. Mumbet manifested her own dreams by brilliantly absorbing the dream of liberty from her oppressors, which was nothing less than the ideals that culminated in the American Declaration of Independence, a major break-through in the evolution of human consciousness. She was free 80 years before the Civil War. No small feat! Some say that she was the first slave freed in the U.S. under the ideals of the constitution.

---

[19] Ibid.
[20] Ibid., pp. 11-12.

I believe that Mumbet and her story are more far-reaching than we know, and possibly outside the realm of the abolition of slavery. For instance, we know that the colonists' meetings affected the actions of Mumbet, but I often wonder about how her powerful life force might have impacted them. Did she contribute to their inspiration?

Mumbet's story is, in one sense, about the ideals of freedom and equality that inspired an oppressed population within another oppressed population. This resulted in a proliferation of higher consciousness during the birth of our nation.

The desperate situation for woman served by Elizabeth Freeman Center and other women's advocacy centers is somewhat analogous. Mumbet's story delivers a message of hope to people who have been victimized. I am grateful to Mumbet for her courage, her creativity and her capacity to find inspiration and manifest dreams in the most dreadful of circumstances! May we all strive for such vision and consciousness to liberate our lives and the lives of others.

Elizabeth Freeman is buried in Stockbridge, MA, and her gravestone reads:

"She was born a slave and remained a slave for nearly thirty years. She could neither read nor write, yet in her own sphere she had no superior nor equal. She neither wasted time nor property. She never violated a trust, nor failed to perform a duty. In every situation of domestic trial, she was the most efficient helper, and the tenderest friend. Good Mother, farewell."[21]

---

[21] Ibid., p. 87.

Chapter 19
Garden in Your Slippers, Paint in Your Pajamas
By Kellie Meisl

I dream of painting and then I paint my dream.
—Vincent Van Gogh

If I had to pick one reason why my journey into the world of dreams began, I would have to say it was due to the birth of my son.

The intimate moments of the days we spent getting acquainted lent naturally to dreamy reflection and afforded me unfettered time to explore some of my life's questions: Where had Benjamin's little Spirit come from and why had it chosen to come to me? More importantly, how could I, his mother, be an instrument of its preservation? In pondering these questions, I realized I needed to reunite with my own Spirit and lead my life in a way that would honor my inner self.

About a year after Benjamin's birth, I began to broach the painful feelings around the emergency c-section I had. It felt traumatic to me that while I was under the fog of general anesthesia, Benjamin had been whisked away in the first moments of his new life, to a cold metal table. He was without the arms and voice of his mother to comfort and reassure him. Exploring my dreams taught me to create rituals to help heal this loss for both of us.

On a warm spring day, before Benjamin's first birthday, I created a little impromptu ceremony for him and me. We sat in a circular garden, Benjamin in my arms. I placed small possessions from generations of our mothers into the circle: an embroidered handkerchief from my maternal grandmother, a tiny fawn pin my mother had worn... I lit a candle and placed the intention for healing the circumstances of Benjamin's birth.

I said a prayer for us and prayed for all of our mothers, for the individual and collective pain they all endured in childbirth throughout the generations. I have faith this helped to produce significant healing. I believe this small ritual established and reaffirmed our spiritual life connection as mother and child. Not long after the ceremony I had this dream:

Plunging and Resurfacing

I am driving along a narrow road with Benjamin in the car. We are surrounded by water on both sides of the car. (I realize in the dream that I have been on this road many times in the past and have always ended the dream intentionally, in fear.) We skid off the right side of the road and plunge into the water. This happens very quickly, but even still, I realize our car is a convertible and we'll have no problem getting out. I try to call for help to a group of people standing nearby but have no voice. I instantly reach for Benjamin who is bundled in a blanket and pull him out. I perform first-aid and clear his mouth and lungs of water. He appears newborn, though in waking life he is a year old. He is sound asleep and remains so, safe, unaffected by the event and not traumatized. My voice returns and I am able to call for help. An ambulance arrives and confirms that we are okay.

The dream ends, but I am able to re-enter the dream consciously.

I am aware that I re-enter the dream and am now looking at the water from a different perspective. I feel no fear. I realize I am now in a narrow canal that contains a round opening where my feet are located. I lie in the water as it rushes all around me and feel revitalized.

It is easy for me to draw parallels between Benjamin's birth and the dream. He is removed from a convertible similar to his removal by c-section. The fact that I have no voice in the dream speaks of the general anesthesia I was under during Benjamin's birth. Benjamin, too, seems to be under general anesthesia as he remains sleeping through the whole event. The fact that I recover him safely from the water and my voice returns signifies to me that the healing ritual I performed has registered healing in my psyche. In the second part of the dream, *I* wait to be reborn. This signifies to me that the birthing experience of my mother is healing, as I had asked for it to be in the ceremony.

I have since used healing rituals in a variety of ways including to honor my dreams. When I have a particularly powerful dream that contains a message, or is one of a recurring theme, I perform a small ritual to thank the dream for coming and to acknowledge its message.

There is a multitude of ways to honor a dream. Creating a piece of art, writing a poem or story are more formal ways to manifest the dream in waking life; lighting a candle, taking a walk or collecting an object in nature are less formal ways. Acting out an aspect of a dream is a particularly efficacious way to bring your dream to life. This can mean connecting with a person in the dream or visiting a place that shows up in a dream.

Examining my dreams has been the most effective way of examining my life. When I find ways to honor my dreams, I find ways to honor my life. Having an awareness of my dream life brings awareness to my everyday life that helps me to feel less fragmented. The dream and life become one and I am whole. Lost parts of me are recovered.

A simple way I honor my dreams is by writing them in a journal. It helps me to keep track of them and they become a story that I can always go back to and reflect upon. Often I notice dream themes emerging. Realizing these themes can be particularly potent in the area of self-discovery. I like to map my themes by writing the theme in the center of a page and writing all associations I can come up with around the outside of the theme. Then, I draw lines to connect associations that seem related. I call this exercise Dream Mapping because the trail of associations, often connected, provide for me a sort of map that gives me clarity and guides me further into exploration. Sometimes I simply write a dream theme on the top of the page of my journal and look up the words in a good standard dictionary. (I have a Webster's International Dictionary, a library edition, written in the 1940's, that I love to use.) I am always amazed what will emerge from these definitions for me. Instinct takes over and that which is *meant to be discovered* will literally leap off the page.

One of the most important things I have learned about working with my dreams is there are no *supposed-tos*. There is no right way to interpret things and no one can tell you what your dreams mean. Time is not linear; the authentic self cannot be squelched. One moves forward automatically, albeit in a seemingly endless spiral of information that has its own rhythm and flow, not a sequence imposed by outside sources. While following my dreams, I walk at my own pace. Sometimes I stumble, sometimes I chase, but I do so with my heart and my outcomes always reveal my Spirit.

By exploring dreams and honoring them I have rekindled my relationship to nature. I am more apt to get outdoors and am more in tune when I do. Animal visitors that come to my dreams will visit me in nature as well. I have come to understand that nature is revealing its story to me and I am more willing to listen. I stroll through my flowers and wade in my backyard brook eagerly awaiting nature's messages. Sometimes I discover beautiful gifts of feathers, eggshells, heart-shaped stones and seeds. It's like the dream is then honoring me.

My gardens have now contained many dream rituals. They have provided a space for me to unfurl my story. I have learned from them and listened to *their* stories. And as with my dreams, I have learned from my gardens that there are no *supposed-tos* in gardening. I may plant something in a specific place only to have it die off and reappear in a new location. When I have thought I can control the look or shape or size of my garden, I am often humbled by the way nature takes over with her own rhythm and harmony, not so unlike my own. Now, many times I find myself digging with bare hands, still in my slippers, without a plan. Sometimes I just need to be patient and let nature reveal itself to me, just as the dreams reveal my true self to me.

By opening myself to my dreams, I have created a portal from which to enter into my creativity. I have found my own style of painting and allowed myself to paint in a variety of places and even in my pajamas. I am learning life is not linear and freedom means breaking the rules and honoring me and my dreams.

Chapter 20
Cycles of Birth and Death:
Shamanic Dream Art and Teaching
By Connie Caldes

Death may be the greatest of all human blessings.
— Socrates

I am able to teach shamanism thanks to sacred power animals, especially Deer and Hummingbird, and a wonderful spirit teacher, my Mohican Grandmother. Power animals assist me when healing others, but Grandmother always shows up to help me find my way. Grandmother instructed me to make turtle rattles. Grandmother gave me my spirit name, Bird Medicine Woman. Grandmother gives me healing images from her cauldron, and Grandmother has taught me to pay attention to the omens of the animals in both my dreams and waking life.

Deer continues to guide me in helping others. Hummingbird reminds me that the world is magical. Bear alerts me when I am with someone who does not have good intentions. Hawk comes to tell me that my medical tests will be OK. Owl informs me of betrayal. Eagle reminds me to fly. And Rattle Snake bites indicate transmutation of my personal chemical state of being, always healing. They all have taught me to teach.

Rattle Snake Bite

I am with my mother. A small baby rattlesnake aligns itself on my spine with its rattle placed on my tailbone and its head lying at navel level. The snake then bites my spine at the navel level, the second chakra, and the place of creation.

When I woke from this dream, I felt quite certain that

something *alchemical* had occurred in my body. Less than one half hour after waking from the dream, my oncologist called. With great excitement, he shared that my CA-15-3 tumor marker had dropped to normal after fifteen months of alarming elevation. I looked online regarding rattlesnake medicine and found that Native Americans associate rattlesnake with healing cancer.

For the past few years, I have continued to create shamanic dream rattles and masks and teach shamanic dream classes, covering many topics of core and contemporary shamanism. In these classes, we have explored our dreams, our ability to create, to recover soul, and to free ourselves of the illusions of this world, all the while intending to raise the vibration of humanity and live in that higher vibration in our own lives. It is a moment-to-moment struggle for all who attempt this path, yet we must if we are to be ready and alert on behalf of opportunity for world healing. Rattles, masks and other sacred objects of art remind us of the need to stay in touch with higher spirit and look to the deepest aspect of our psyches for answers to our everyday concerns. We live in a world full of suffering. We hope that our work inspires all that come in contact with it to create their own sacred world, including artistic projects, and relieve their own suffering.

When we create, we move a piece of our inner world into a space that can be perceived by those around us. Something unknown is manifested and teaches of the beauty within the creator. It also gives form and meaning to the dreams and stories carried by that individual. It encourages others to be creators and to bring meaning and healing to their own lives. Creating rattles has become a way for me to both heal myself and help others heal themselves.

This magic occurred when participants in my shamanic classes created masks to honor their helping spirits. The front of the mask became an artistic creation for each member of the group. Furthermore, upon empowering the masks with the helping spirits through ritual, the masks taught that they were in fact a living being in their own right.

We placed the masks on the opposite side of the room with the finished side facing away. We then lit up the inner masks with small candles to look into the being that resided in each mask. The masks came alive in a manner that shocked each member of the group. We could perceive life and power in each mask within the framework of the shape of the face upon which the mask was created, the individual participant. The spirits spoke through the masks once we opened the space for their presence. Furthermore, the masks taught each member of the group that the depth of being is not within reach of the everyday human mind, that we are so much more than we understand, and that at our core we are compassion.

Since being diagnosed with breast cancer in early 2002, I have experienced several cycles of birth and death by metaphorical definition. Firstly, the experience of cancer itself brought me through every imaginable and conceivable feeling of both joy and sorrow. Making a choice to try to heal and recover from the cancer was more challenging than I had imagined, for to go after life, we must risk confrontation with death. Furthermore, the immense changes that accompany these initiations are not palatable for some friends, and one loses and gains many relationships. In my experience, it was all for the better despite the pain that these changes cause. Secondly, my husband and I decided to separate, which resulted in further tumultuous life changes, including seeing my children through the pain and suffering of divorce, moving out of our home, seeking employment and surviving the legal process which favors masculine values. At times, the pain was so great, it was hard to move forward, and normal day-to-day joy was severely thwarted. However, I learned to keep my eye on the proverbial light at the end of the tunnel, a symbol of both life and death. I am certain that my encounters with both literal and metaphorical death have made me a better teacher than I might have been without those experiences.

When we looked into the gentle wisdom of the spirit masks, we saw something unimagined, something greater than ourselves, something worth striving for. We are here, in part, to grow into all that we can be, beings of compassion, love, generosity, support, trust and integrity.

The masks were not created on the same person, yet the expressions deep within each reflected peace and harmony, of both humanity and something beyond, beyond our wildest dreams.

Chapter 21
Conscious Power: Using Life's Metaphors
By Kellie Meisl

It is a miracle that curiosity survives formal education.
— Albert Einstein

If the dream is a translation of waking life, waking life is also a translation of the dream.
— Rene Margritte

I am contemplating returning to my job as a teacher. This is something I have considered frequently in the past decade of my teaching hiatus. When I was a teacher, I taught in a local inner-city school and I envisioned that I would return there to do my work again someday. Yet, I have interviewed there twice in the past five years but did not receive a position. I do not understand this from a practical standpoint. My tenure as a teacher there was successful; my evaluations were exemplary. I was passionate about teaching children in those days. I would spend hours before and after school and on weekends building upon the structure of the curricula with ideas that would come to me spontaneously. I would formulate lessons that were intricately connected to the needs of each student; this process would culminate in group learning, with each child contributing their part to the whole. My lessons incorporated hands-on activities, movement, music, diversity and creativity. I welcomed guests into the classroom, including parents with whom I formed bonds. I offered before school, lunch and after school programs for my students. I provided home visits. I was living my life's purpose with enthusiasm.

I resigned from my position just five years into it, to become a stay at home mom for my first and only child. It was a tough decision to put my career on hold but I felt it was the right thing for me and for my son. Just as I had cared deeply about the well being of the children I had taught, I felt a strong calling to the responsibility of being a mom. I was not convinced that I could carry out both jobs with the focus they each required, so I chose the job of mother.

Over the past summer, I spoke with yet another new principal about the possibility of coming back to my old school. He told me he had no openings, but he assured me he would let me know if anything opened up; we would talk then, he had said. I remember having a gut reaction to his words: he did not know my passion and though he said otherwise, it was not in his plan to learn about me. My service at that school seemed to evaporate into another place in time and space.

It was my friend Kathryn who kept encouraging me to return to the work she had once been witness to. Yet, each time I prepared for the process of returning, I would have dreams where I could not get in the door, literally. Or, I'd be in a maze somewhere in the school and couldn't find my way. One time, I didn't have the right pencil for the test. Yet, somehow the dreams would also present me as a teacher, as though I got in through the back door somehow.

In Through the Back Door

I am rambling around in the lobby of the school I used to teach in. I am unable to go either into the school further, or out of the school. I try different doorways but have no luck with moving beyond the lobby itself. One doorway I enter leads me to a playground style slide, curved and plastic. I take the slide but find myself deposited right back to the lobby. I just cannot get anywhere, no matter how hard I try. I realize I must leave. But, the front doors are locked and I cannot leave through them, I will have to leave through the backdoor...

The Odds are Stacked

I am at the old school where I used to teach. I am about to be administered a standardized test. I am with a group, including the principal and several other males. I am concerned about the test because I was not shown any of the criteria that will be on the test ahead of time and therefore feel at a disadvantage for taking the test. The others in the room seem to be aware of the nature of the test. I cannot find a writing utensil, and then my friend Kathryn, who has appeared, gives me a pink pencil.

And then it happened, I did get in, *through the back door*, and the dreams continued to present themselves, for real. In the fall of 2008, Kathryn encouraged me to take on a regular part-time substitute teacher job for a teacher with whom I had taught previously. She had become ill and would need a regular sub from time to time. As was normal protocol, the teacher could arrange for her own substitute. Kathryn was close to both of us and felt this would be a good fit. Ironically, I would be teaching in the very classroom I had always taught in while at the school. It did *seem* to be a good fit. Yet the nagging feeling of the dreams, that something wasn't quite right, emerged shortly after my decision to return. I kept pushing the feelings away though, assuming that they were the self-doubt I originally had when I questioned if I would have enough energy to teach and be a mother. My mind and body seemed to be saying: *You do not belong here; it would require too many sacrifices.* I didn't want to hear that voice so I tried to suppress it. Then the dream began appearing each time I would enter the school, bringing with it all the answers I needed; the only requirement: pay attention and read the signs.

The dream came alive in the theme of walls when I began subbing. At first, everything seemed fine, albeit I was slightly rusty. I felt I was getting back in the groove and the students were responding well to me. The only thing that stood out to me that was any different, was that the gray film that once covered every window that lined one wall of the classroom in which I once taught, was now gone. The film had come from a most unfortunate mistake on the part of the installers when the school had been built; they had forgotten to remove the protective plastic coating. Once the windows were in, the coating had baked on in the sun. This wound up obstructing the view to the outdoors almost completely except for a cloudy light that managed to shine through. The years I taught there we had hung a window feeder for the birds, but we could only see their shadows as they fed, yet it still brought the children and me some joy. The new view was now vivid and lovely, probably the best view in the whole school, revealing gloriously colored Fall Mountains hovering over the cityscape. It made me feel *clear* that I would know if teaching was going to fit again into my life.

Then the next wall showed up: it came in the form of the new principal and his freshly painted walls. He presented himself *as* a wall to me. He had painted many walls in the school a deep blue over the summer, a job he took upon himself. The color showed itself as powerful; the walls now demanded attention. On the day the wall had shown up, I was at the school on my own time, getting ready to participate in a walking trip with Kathryn's class. I got off of the elevator and as I walked by one of the new blue walls in the principal's open office, my eye caught him. The principal was wearing a blue shirt identical to the color of the wall. I knew it was a sign: *he* was part of the wall. This might have had some positive connotations to it, walls are boundaries, walls are protective, yet the feelings I had about this dream seemed to be presented this way: walls were meant to keep something out. The image hung with me.

The next time I subbed, the walls were presented everywhere. I was told early in the morning that the boys' bathroom in the area where I was teaching would be closed. Two young male students had written extreme graffiti on the bathroom walls and were being made by the principal to paint over it immediately. For many reasons, this school was full of defiant children. They lived in a tough neighborhood, one of addiction, crime and dysfunction. Many of the students were deprived of connection and support. Though they were only in elementary school, they often got themselves ready and out the door in the morning, sometimes in ripped clothes, many times without breakfast. They were starved in other ways too, including for attention. No doubt this act of defiance on the part of the boys was just that, a call for attention. One of my strengths as a teacher in this school had been that I could read between the lines of behavior and get to the nugget of what the children were trying so desperately to speak, their truth. I did not take their defiance at face value. I looked below the surface and strived to address it in its fuller forms.

Something had me uneasy this day about the fact that these boys were taken out of their learning environment so readily and made to cover the problem so quickly. Yet, it looked like a natural consequence to a "bad" behavior that had occurred. My head was being given one story about the writing on the wall, while my heart was feeling another.

Later in the day I decided to trust my instincts when I began teaching the math lesson for the third graders and decided to bring them outdoors. It was a beautiful, sunny fall day. The children were to be reviewing parallel and perpendicular lines. What better place to examine these lines at play than around the school building and playground? This is one of my teaching practices: bring students outside the walls. And so I did. The normally tired math period was renewed with enthusiasm and even joy. What transpired was a one hundred percent team effort. Children enthusiastically discovered, pointed out, and recorded example after example of parallel and perpendicular lines. Not surprisingly, many lines were found along the exterior walls. At one point, a couple of students pointed out the perpendicular lines of the letter *H* sprayed in black paint along a cement wall. The initial instinct to launch into a defensive posture about the vandalism was quickly overridden by the realization that these were the perpendicular lines of their world: there was no wrong in this moment, only innocence. Graffiti or no graffiti.

On the next day I subbed, one of the little boys in the class, considered to have special needs, brought the wall dream alive again. The wisdom he imparted to me blew me away. I was having trouble understanding schedules and new procedures. No one had come in to discuss this with me or help me out with this in any official way. I was there but invisible to the other adults in the building except to my friend Kathryn and a particularly kind and helpful part-time assistant teacher. By now, the principal had made his way through the halls that outlined the open classroom without stopping to say hello on a couple of occasions, so it was clear to me that other than receiving help from the caring assistant teacher, I would not be given formal instruction on the workings of the school. So when little Lance came to me upon overhearing my confusion around some procedures and pointed out that every procedure was actually posted on walls all around the school, (in fact many, many messages handed down by administration were now all over the walls), if one bothered to notice them, I was bowled over. He was right: *the writing was on the wall*! I learned to pay even more attention to what was *on* the walls. (What I saw were many strong belief statements, in the form of posters, about excellence, expectations and organization.) I now *knew* this story needed to be written.

Something else presented itself to me, the message of one of my bedside visitors in a previous dream: "You write the words, I'll provide the illustrations."

Now I was beginning to understand that my creativity was being channeled into telling the story. I was feeling I had a purpose.

Then I had another sleeping dream:

Healing Old Wounds

I see Nan, a deceased teacher who recently passed. She enters the room taller and leaner than she was in real life. She is limber and flexible in her movements. She is wearing an asymmetrical dress made of beige feathers. She does a unique dance, extending her left leg upward. The other people in the room, woman teachers she once worked with, ooooo and ahhhh at her dance moves.

The dream changes and I am subbing for Lilly. The classroom I am in is in the school where I once taught. It has no walls; it is a big open space (as it was when the school was first built; it is an open classroom.) The children have moved all of the furniture and the floor is an open space of new green carpet. The children are all crowded into the right hand corner of the room, to the right of where I sit upon the floor. Space is all around me.

The dream changes again and I am watching a dark-skinned little boy whose left foot has been badly damaged; he cannot walk. However, he can ride a bicycle. He pedals off and I marvel at how well he can balance and work both pedals. I feel that though he is wounded, this talent will serve him well.

This dream, about walls, space, balance and overcoming obstacles can definitely be a metaphor for what is currently happening in my life. It seems to be a mirror image of how I feel when I am actually teaching in the classroom. In this dream, walls are not an issue; they do not exist. The space is open; I am on a green new turf. I have all the space I need. Obstacles are no longer around me. The teacher performs a dance and is admired by her peers. I receive the gift of *seeing* that the wounded child has learned coping mechanisms and will be able to move forward through life; he has learned balance and this will help him on his journey. I am also struck by the asymmetry of the teacher's dress and the imbalance of the little boy's feet. This dream seems to be presenting both *sides* of a story; it presents the right and the left. Reflected back to me is the reverence I feel for the learning process: for the teacher who has learned to dance, and for the child who has learned to balance. This is the same enthusiasm I used to feel every time I entered the classroom, before the walls started to appear.

I also cannot help but to wonder if the possibility of the wounded dark child striking a balance may be a precognitive message about the presidential election that is to happen in a few weeks, our first black candidate to make it to the final two, is *running*. Will he *balance and heal* the wounds of America by receiving the office?

The next time I return to the classroom, I have an opposite experience of that in my dream. The classroom feels crowded. The makeshift walls, bookcases and furniture placed down the center of the room that give the feeling of division around this open classroom, are very pronounced to me. Everywhere, unnatural juxtapositions of furniture seem daunting to negotiate. There are gaps in the fabricated wall and the teacher next-door leaps through them on occasion to admonish the children in my classroom. That day there are many adult visitors in the classroom, including the principal. He comes in and seats himself at the computer in the room, *to my left*. I realize he is there to meet with the other teachers on the team only as they begin to file in. I am talking with the children as we pick up from the morning goings-on before they go to lunch. At first, I am confused by the principal's presence and ask him if he needs me, but he shakes his head no. I still receive no verbal contact; it is the fifth time I have been in this school, the third time he has been in my close proximity; he still does not speak.

In the afternoon as we get ready for math, the children are antsy and moody. The kind-hearted assistant teacher jokes that in this classroom, we really only have one wall to climb if we need to. I look at the wall, it has always been my favorite wall there, a big black chalkboard of a wall that I fill with lots of colorful chalk words and illustrations for the children, it's not been a bad wall for me to climb; it is a wall I will probably climb again one day but I am convinced by now it will not be here. I stare down at my boots and the words, *you can't go back* comes to mind. I must admit, I do feel a bit defeated on this day.

The last time I am set to sub, I get a call saying that it turns out I am not needed. A replacement will be in for me instead, no real explanation given, just that she was already going to be there. I am not sure what this means, but I am clear on the greater meaning for me: *the writing is on the wall.*

It is with a mixture of wistfulness for what might have been and a great sense of relief that I can return to being the mom, volunteer, artist and writer that I had been before becoming the temporary teacher. I feel a freedom I had not recognized before taking the substitute position. Before returning to the classroom, I had contained my views, believing I needed to return to a traditional job as a teacher to be successful. I know now, through this experience of living the dream, that this is not the case. I do not need to be defined according to the terms within that box. That will not take me in the direction of my truest dream. My path, no matter how divergent it is at times, is my own path and someone else's walls cannot impose it upon me.

I sit one Saturday morning with my friend Maureen; we are in Connie's dream room and Maureen asks the question, "Do you think people can have precognitive dream experiences while they are awake?" "Absolutely," I say. I tell her I am writing this story. I look forward to sharing it with her.

Just yesterday, America elected its first black president, Barack Obama. Talk about overcoming obstacles and breaking through walls! I sit all goose bumpy and tingling listening to his acceptance speech. In it he reminds us we must each rebuild America *brick by brick*, using our hands, just as our ancestors did before us. I am reminded of the brick walls the students examined in the hands-on math lesson we did together. I am also reminded of the walls of a castle I recently volunteered to help build. We turned aluminum soda cans into bricks and used them as building blocks that we assembled brick by brick to build our walls. This was a project I organized with the PTO at my son Benjamin's school. We built a float for our local Halloween parade. My dream of designing a *green* float made of recyclable materials had come to me spontaneously and manifested. *(Like the green spacious carpet of my dream, I am reminded that I will have green, fertile areas where my teaching can continue.)* Some people said it couldn't be done, building with cans, but we did it and it turned out spectacularly thanks to a team effort. We were a group of people who welcomed each other and chose to work together and support one another, for a common good. The cans were donated to the Lion's Club when we were through. What a difference this makes: performing your service where you are wanted.

Not long after I had another dream:

Purple Pen

I am in an old house of a wealthy young woman and her father. I am in my twenties and am with a group of others my age. We are here to learn something. An older woman of higher learning will come to tell us our truths. We each have pen-shaped objects in our hands. Our truths are based on these objects that we must present them to her when she comes. We ascend the old stairs of the house to a room where the learning is to take place. As I ascend, I notice the rust colored carpet is old and worn; it is dusty too. The father who lives there uses this worn path, in the center of the stairs, to ascend to his bedroom, where he is right now. His room is at the top of the stairs on the left. I can see his footprints; I walk alongside them to the right, in the dust. Then, I walk down a long hall to the learning room; it is on the right. The hallway is carpeted in olive green and has a brown water spot on the left side of the hall, across from the learning room. When I am in the learning room, we talk as a group awaiting the old woman's arrival. A couple of young males who are present are confused about a poetry assignment. I share with them a simple way of looking at the concept of poetry and then recite a quick poem about my right arm as I hold it up. Soon after, I realize I have forgotten my pen-shaped object downstairs. I descend downstairs automatically, materializing on the bottom step and find my pen in the crevice of the stair, in the carpet. The pen is light lavender in color. I stare at it for a while trying to understand what this pen means to me...

As I write this dream story, I am struck once again by the balance and contrast. The dream is full of new and old. I find myself wondering if I am both the young wealthy woman and the wise old woman. I note the ascent and descent of the steps. The rustiness of the carpet reminds me of feeling rusty when I taught in the classroom. Yet, I take an unworn path to get to the place of higher learning. In the learning room, I am both a teacher and a learner. I find the teaching easy; I can make sense of the complex, simply. I forget my tool for revealing the higher truth and I must descend to find it, it is a quick descent and I materialize rapidly. I locate my tool wedged between the first and second step. In the dream, I recite a poem about my right arm, my writing arm. I am struck by this revelation. Is the dream telling me I am to be both a teacher and a learner through my writing? Perhaps this is why the old classroom is presenting me walls. Maybe it is time to blend the old with the new. *I know the wise woman is coming to claim my purple pen; I must not lose it.*

Segue to spring of 2009. I am teaching again. I teach in an upstairs room at the local municipal art center, located in the heart of the city. Yes, dusty old carpeted stairs lead to the hall and room where I am teaching. I enjoy teaching classes I designed by integrating art and dreams. A woman in my group resembles the wise older woman of my dream, another, the eager student. In some ways I am the wise woman too, imparting what I have learned onto them. It is a perfect balance. Often, when the class is over, I stare out the large windows that line the walls of the room I teach in; the cityscape surrounds me and I feel in awe of this magical space.

Sometimes walls hinder our dreams. Other times walls will lead us to follow our dreams. Sometimes dreams will flow in a circuitous way, leading us seemingly around and around without pointing out the obvious. Sometimes dreams are relentless in delivering their message. Sometimes dreams will lead us through the back door. But always dreams carry with them the metaphors within our lives. We just need to pay attention.

Chapter 22
The Mosaic Medicine Man: Dream Doctors
By Kellie Meisl

*The art of medicine consists of amusing the patient while
nature cures the disease.*
— Voltaire

*I am in a college dormitory, joined by three female friends
from high school. I am not comfortable in the clothes I have
on. I cannot find the right clothes to wear; style, color, and
comfort all elude me. I go back to my childhood home to find
some clothes but can only find black clothing. I reason I will
take these black clothes with me, as at least they are a neutral
color, though they aren't particularly comfortable or stylish.
This bothers me. I have another option; I can wear a plaid
green uniform, but I am not able to "get the uniform right."
The skirt is frayed at the edges.*

*Then, I am back at the dorm. I stand in the "common
area" with the three high school, now college, friends. Other
females are nearby in this expansive room. From the far wall,
to my right, I see a small man emerge; he is standing and
riding on the back of a large beetle. The man is about three
feet tall and has "mosaic" skin; dark tattoo ink colors of blue,
green and red form shapes, in random geometric patterns,
over his face and body. He carries a bow and arrow. The
beetle is black, hard-shelled and the size of a large tortoise.
The mosaic skinned man glides with ease and balance on the
large insect's flat back, in slow rhythmic strides across the
room. They stop; the mosaic man stares directly into my eyes;
his eyes are soft electric blue. He draws back his bow and let's
his arrow fly; it strikes my throat with alarming precision,
and the tiny tan beads of my necklace sprinkle to the floor.*

As I rewrite this nine-year-old dream that is with me as

vividly now as the day I had it, I am about to take my morning medicine, Synthroid, a synthetic hormone replacement for an inactive thyroid that I have taken faithfully every day for the past thirteen years. Through the years, the little pill has come in a variety of pastel colors and has been both circular and oval-shaped as dosages and brands have been moderated and swapped. This morning, the pill I am about to take is a tiny, round, tan one, as were the beads that fell from my neck in the dream. The medication I was taking at the time of the dream almost a decade ago was tan and round and tiny as well. I noted the similarity of the medication to the necklace immediately after awaking from the dream; I am pleasantly amused that *a bead* is sitting beside my coffee cup as I write; this is quite unplanned. I am reminded of a recurring childhood dream that contained little figures in pastel colors.

Pastel Aliens

I am a child of age four. I am at my grandparent's home in Vermont. It is a place where I am loved and comfortable. I am playing in the back yard when these little pastel aliens, no taller than I land. I run in to my grandparent's home and try to get my grandmother or grandfather to listen to me as I tell them of the intruders. They cannot hear me. My parents are there and they do not hear me either. The dream repeats on many nights. After several recurrences of the dream, I discover my great-uncle Frank inside my grandparent's home upon running indoors away from the pastel aliens. This time he can hear me; he is the only one. He brings me outside and shows me how to round the little fellows into a pile. He then shows me how, by jumping on the pile, I can spring free and fly, hovering above the chaos of the colorful little intruders. He also shows me how to use my arms as wings.

At the time of the Mosaic Man dream, I was pretty sure about a few of its messages. One, my *Synthroid* and the necklace I wore in the dream were connected. Two, I was having a recurring dream theme, which was: *not having the right clothes to wear, not feeling comfortable in the clothes I was in*. And three, the little mosaic man, as I called him from day one, was a medicine man of sorts; he had a message for me and it was directly related to my health. Later I would realize this dream would have a never ending, unfolding quality to it, always willing to supply one more piece of my psyche when I was ready to see it.

Segue to the clothes dream theme: this has been a recurring *life* theme for me as well. Quite often, particularly from pre-adolescence through my early twenties, with shorter bouts in my thirties and even fewer in my forties, thankfully, I have found myself uncomfortable in my own clothes. When this was occurring frequently, I felt my clothing was not exactly on par with what everybody else was wearing, namely my school friends. So I can see where this dream was heading. When I was growing up I often felt like my clothes did not fit properly. Sometimes my clothing discomfort emerged because I just too plainly plagiarized somebody else's style for my own good. However, sometimes I was, and am now, truly satisfied in my own clothes, pleasantly content putting together all the pieces of my look and revealing the real me in the process. On these occasions I note, my outfits often seem to have some sort of vintage element in the mix, reminding me of my reverie for things past.

Revisiting this dream now burrows me to a deeper layer: my discomfort with my clothes also reflects a discomfort with being in my own skin. Dreams and skin both have layers. Certainly, the little man's skin was vividly accentuated in my dream, a not-so-hidden hint, I realize. Also, what I did not know then is that two years after the dream, my own skin would exhibit color changes, a byproduct of my autoimmune disease, of which I have three (three friends in the dream, three autoimmune diseases). Some of my normal melanocytes, producers of pigment in skin, have been destroyed by my overzealous immune system that sees them as invaders instead of friendly cells. Now I am a two-toned person, mostly light tan but with some white irregular shapes on parts of my body, predominantly my hands, feet, lower legs and lower arms. Was this part of what the little man was alluding to when he shot my medication from my throat? Was he telling me that, within my autoimmune disease, there were more symptoms to come? Was he preparing me in some way? My challenge to feel comfortable in my own skin had now become *visible* to me. The dream seemed to be saying: "I will give you a visual metaphor for what is to come."

I wondered right away too if my throat region, the aim of the diminutive, tattooed fellow, was connected to the dream. I was pretty sure it was. In the eastern model of health, the throat is located in the fifth chakra, a spinning wheel of energy associated with expressing oneself and one's willpower. This area also contains the thyroid gland, a modulating system for the way one's body is regulated and metabolizes hormones and even nutrition and body rhythms. Was this dream about becoming aware of how I express myself in relation to my thyroid disease? Clothing is certainly an expression of self. Doubting oneself, as I did my wardrobe in the dream, reflects a lack of faith and trust in one's ability to express oneself accurately and go with the flow. It is true, speaking up and sharing what I believe in has been a long process for me. And now, having made the connection to the dream of the colorful pastel little men, I can begin to see the origin of my personal myth, one in which I learned that it is difficult to speak up and be heard by those who are larger than you. I am grateful I kept trying and that my uncle Frank heard me and taught me how to fly. I was able to thank him for that not so long ago, before he passed, when I now had my own child.

Speaking one's truth can come in many forms. Sometimes without knowing it, we reveal the truth of ourselves to the world. We show who we are in our words, in our actions, in the clothes we wear; our truth is the design of who we are. Our patterns can cut deep like the tattooed lines of the mosaic man's skin. Often we live with a lack of awareness of the routines we have habitually established. I believe our dreams present our true essence. The key is we must be open to the images in our dreams then we will have the freedom of observation. If we receive a message about a direction we are going in life that feels uncomfortable or worn out, we have the option to reconfigure our life. It takes some examination at first, and we must go beyond the skin-deep aspects of ourselves to do so. Our dreams are an ever deep well that leads us straight to the heart of ourselves, although we must sometimes be willing to lower ourselves into the cavernous regions of our subconscious to find *us*. Ironically, in the dark regions of the well, we will find the golden light of self; the *real truth* of who we are awaits us.

Nine years after the dream, I am now able to see that the black of my childhood clothing is a portal inviting me back to the well, to be lowered into those places in my subconscious. There I can bring to the surface the little girl whom bought into having to look, speak and act a certain way. She and I will need to reexamine some old beliefs that no longer serve us. She wasn't very thick skinned early on as I recall, or is that too just another belief that grew into my tissue without consent? I know this: I can look at my skin now and embrace it, its emerging patterns, all new to me, reflect back a lightening up of my spirit. The young woman I was in high school or college might not have been able to take these changes as easily, the emerging wise woman is in awe of them. Granted, there are days when I just want to fit in and look like everybody else. But there are also days when I feel blessed to have been given this mark, manifested all the way from a dream, a visual gift validating that the dream and life are one, a single continuum where soul resides and speaks to us if we are willing to listen, bringing us mosaic medicine men when we need them.

Chapter 23
Dreaming a Field of Dreams: Precognition and Family Dynamics
By Connie Caldes

A sweet thing, for whatever time,
to revisit in dreams the dear dad we have lost.
—Euripides

John is the father of my childhood friend, Marie. John grew up with my father. They played baseball together many decades ago on a prestigious high school all-star team. They were both considered bound for the major leagues; however, both opted for professional graduate school instead. They remain friendly, but they both have regrets about abandoning their baseball dreams.

My paternal grandfather died in the mid-seventies. Sometime, during the latter part of 1988 while I was in my late twenties, I had the following dream:

A Visit to Dad's Heyday (Late 1988)

I am with John. He tells me that he is going to take me back in time so that I can watch my father play baseball. We are immediately transferred to a baseball field in my father's hometown. John vanishes. I am positioned between Home Plate and First Base. I look up and see the sixteen-year-old version of my father at Shortstop. I am quite surprised at seeing the younger version of him. The game progresses and I watch every fluid move that my father makes. He is an incredible athlete! Then I notice someone pacing between Third Base and Home Plate. It is my paternal grandfather. He is upset about my father. He knows that the baseball field is a safe haven for my father, but underneath this mask of

167

confidence, lays a hurt young man. He has not recovered from the early loss of his mother, my grandmother. My grandfather is fretting about what to do. Everyone disappears and I sit on home plate and sob.

During the final months of 1988, and after the above dream, my brother and I decided that we would talk to my father in the hopes of bringing the historical family pain into the light and encourage healing. The loss of my grandmother has left my father's generation with much sadness. My brother and I were concerned and hoped that we could make a difference. My father's two sisters wrote to my father. My brother and I discussed our family history many times; and, when recommended by a counselor, we worked on letters to our father to describe our impressions. We were careful to filter out any issues we carried about our own childhood and family experiences, as this was not the proper forum for such expression. We did not want to provoke guilt and shame about some of the fallout of the loss of our grandmother as it might actually prevent healing. I had a terrible time getting clear on what I wanted to say in my letter. I had difficulty expressing my feelings without the presence of blame because I felt that my father was hard on me, and that some of that had to do with my grandmother. When my brother and I were done with our writing, I had a mediocre letter that did not feel good to me. It was not from the heart. I went home very upset about the process and wondered if I should back out. A few nights before we were to meet with my father, I went to sleep and dreamed:

Grandfather Intervenes (Early January 1989)

I find myself sitting in a small circle of chairs. Then, I notice that my brother is also present. I think, "Oh my God – we are here to talk to my father." I am surprised that it has come so soon. I thought that I had more time to prepare. I see an empty chair across the circle. I think, "That chair is for my

*father." Suddenly, the door to the room flies open and my
paternal grandfather enters. I am shocked. He pulls the empty
chair towards me and sits down right in front of me. I say,
"What are you doing here? You are DEAD!" He says, "I know.
I have come in spirit to be part of this. I have come to tell you
that you are doing the right thing. Please tell your father that I
came and that I always worried about him and his pain.
Please tell him." He grabs my shoulders and emphasizes that I
must talk to my father about the loss of his mother. I shoot out
of bed and grab my husband. I tell him that my grandfather
came. I tell my husband "it was so real, I could smell him."*

In early January of 1989, my brother and I arrived at my
father's house. I was frightened. I feared that my father was not
going to hear me about the impact of family history and pain. I
feared that he would be angry because he is a private person.
My brother and I entered our father's living room to share our
letters. When my turn came, I put down my letter and told my
father my dream of his father. He teared up while I told him. It
seemed that he believed that my grandfather had spoken to me.
I left knowing that I had done my best. I had given my father
the gift that I truly had to give, a loving message from his own
beloved (and much missed) father.

If You Build It, He Will Come[22] (Waking Dream, Later in
1989)

*Several months later, I go to the movies with my mother,
brother and husband. The movie is the "Field of Dreams."
Naturally, I like the movie because I was raised to love
baseball. The surprise does not come until the end of the film.
The father of the Kevin Costner role shows up at Home Plate to
greet his son. The father is his younger self, the younger self*

---

[22] Phil Alden Robinson, Director, *Field of Dreams*, 1989.

that his son never knew. They finally have a chance to heal the wounds between them. In a fleeting moment, it hits me hard that I am in my dream and in the experience of the meeting with my father. I look at my husband. He is sobbing over his own father loss issues. At a moment that finally seems appropriate, I say to my husband, "Do you remember my dream about going back in time to watch my father play baseball?" He remembers but does not grasp my level of excitement about this. I leave the theater blown away by this powerful coincidence.

Since this powerful experience, I have maintained a sense of my grandfather's presence. He comes and goes, but is particularly present at important moments:

A Visit from My Grandfather (Waking Dream, November, 1999)

I am in a spiritual workshop at The Monroe Institute. As directed, I take a silent walk in nature. I decide to spend time in the Labyrinth that Robert Monroe constructed in honor of his wife, Nancy Penn. I have made my way to the center and am spiraling my way out. My stride abruptly changes to one that I recognize as my grandfather's. I have a sense of him moving through me, from the back to the front of my body. The message that I receive is that he continues to watch over me and that he is at peace with my choice to pursue my spiritual dreams.

He has come many times since...

Chapter 24
Golden Greek: Chrisoula's Story:
Confronting Family Secrets
By Connie Caldes

We can easily forgive a child who is afraid of the dark; the real tragedy of life is when men are afraid of the light.
— Plato

My Greek grandmother, Chrisoula Caldes, died on January 24, 1952. She was fifty-two years old. I was born four days short of eight years later. My first cousins and I never knew her, even those cousins that were born before she died. Her three children, Connie, Helen, and Teddy found it difficult to talk about her life, so those of us in the next generation were left with many questions about what had happened to her.

My father, Theodore George, Chrisoula's son and youngest child, was born on October 16, 1930 and does not remember much about her. Only that she made him wear shoes that were too tight and that she once scolded him when he tripped on the sidewalk, telling him that God was reminding him that he had done something naughty earlier that day. He often told my brother George and me that his mother died when he was eighteen years old, but he was actually 21 years old. I always wondered why my father called himself "The Golden Greek."

My Aunt Helen, the middle child, born on January 2, 1928, speaks more freely of her mother. She says that Chrisoula became depressed when my grandfather lost his thriving Greek restaurant business, The Caldes Restaurant, in Albany, NY, in 1933, during the Great Depression. She says that Chrisoula withdrew into a saddened and quiet state. Helen's children, my first cousins, are Ronald, Richard and Melissa.

My Aunt Connie, the oldest child, born on March 17, 1923, suffered greatly at the early loss of her mother to a mental institution. She had been left to care for her two younger siblings under great duress. She also finds the subject of Chrisoula difficult to broach, but does so more freely now in the twilight of her own life. Connie's children are my first cousins, Cathy, George and John.

I recently was gifted, from my Aunt Connie's son George, with my grandmother's record from the Hudson River State Hospital in Poughkeepsie, NY. The two-inch stack of paperwork is a fourteen-year chronicle of Chrisoula's life and doings during the time period from 1938 until 1952. The record is full of details from interviews with Chrisoula by clinicians and medical data regarding her treatment. The record was not easy to read, for my cousin George or for me, for what happened to Chrisoula is not tolerable to the imagination of those who loved her during those years, or to those of us who did not know her, her grandchildren. Both George and I cry and grieve each time we look deeper into her story.

It occurred to me that I should put her to rest in a meaningful and healing way for our family. My cousin George believes that I should. It occurred to me that what we knew of her life and gifts was not enough. She was a beautiful human being who needed help, but the help that she was given, the best medicine known during her times, was dreadful and barbaric. It is amazing that she survived as long as she did. She endured fourteen years of hell in her private world in that hospital. She longed to go home and be with her husband and children. She tried. She meant to. Many who loved her, including my grandfather, wrote passionate letters, pleading for a cure for her and her release from the asylum for over a decade, to no avail. My grandfather's endearing term for her was "Malama," meaning "Pure Gold." The record shows a devoted husband who agonized over the loss of his beloved wife and grieved for the intense pain of his children. He would have gone to any length to save her.

Nancy Chodorow reflects my intention in this writing in *The Power of Feelings*, from the writings of Hans Loewald on the benefit of transferring unconscious meaning to conscious phenomena, turning ghosts into ancestors:

"Ghosts of the unconscious will *taste blood* and awaken when they sense something familiar in conscious and preconscious life - the day residues that enable dream formation, for example. But as Loewald puts it 'those who know ghosts tell us that they long to be released from their ghost life and led to rest as ancestors. As ancestors they live forth in the present generation, while as ghosts they are compelled to haunt the present generation with their shadow life. Transference is pathological insofar as the unconscious is a crowd of ghosts... [In analysis] ghosts of the unconscious, imprisoned by defenses but haunting the patient in the dark of his defenses and symptoms, are allowed to taste blood, are let loose.'"[23]

There is a gaping and bleeding wound in the body of my family. The ghost of Chrisoula resides in that wound. We need to heal the wound by accepting the truth of Chrisoula's demise while painting healing images of her story on our collective soul. The secret of Chrisoula's suffering must be brought into the light in order for us to move on. My father's generation still mourns for her loss; but they do not know what to mourn, for they do not know the truth of what she endured or the depth of who she was. Too much about her is misunderstood and left unspoken. She did not have a chance to speak. Her gifts have

---

[23] Nancy Chodorow, *The Power of Feelings: Personal Meaning in Psychoananlysis, Gender, and Culture* (New Haven: Yale University Press, 1999) 245-6.

been lost in the family's need to cover the wound with stories and fables that were put in place to help them survive the trauma of losing her. The record of Chrisoula's years in Poughkeepsie speaks many unspoken truths.

Dear Dad, Aunt Connie and Aunt Helen:

I write this piece as I take dream journeys to find Chrisoula's voice so that our family might turn Chrisoula's ghost into an ancestor. She is our ancestor. We shall no longer be haunted, but rather guided by the gifts of an unknown endearing woman named Chrisoula, meaning golden, interpreted as the affectionate "Goldie." We shall let her shine her golden light upon us from the heavens. And finally, we might say fair well to our lost mother.

Love,
Connie

Greek Days

Chrisoula Caldes was born in 1900, daughter of Peter Chaconas and Fatula Contogone. She had a younger sister and brother, Sophia and Thomas, each of whom lived to be over one hundred years old. Her genetics would say that she was meant to live a long and healthy life, but she had a painful childhood in Greece, and I believe that this rocky foundation was at the core of her issues later in life.

First, when Chrisoula was eight years old, her mother died of Tuberculosis. This early and traumatic loss in her life broke her heart. Later on, even Chrisoula would tell those that tried to help her that she never got over the loss of her mother. And what made it much worse was that her father married a woman who set Chrisoula and her siblings to hard work. Chrisoula grew up as a Cinderella child, holding onto hopes and dreams of a much better future.

In 1918, at the age of eighteen, Chrisoula had an attack of the "fever" and a brush with death. This illness may have brought back her mother's death and touched much of her inner fear, leaving her all the more fragile.

I cannot help but wonder what she felt like as a young girl?

Chrisoula Speaks:

I was in pain when my mother died. I missed her dearly and believed that she had joined my ancestors in the stars. I would look out the window at night and try to see her, but I could not. I felt despair. I wanted to go with her, to go where she went, but could not. My stepmother was cruel to me. She was angry because she thought that my father loved my mother more than he loved her. She was right about that, and she knew that I knew. So, she hated me, and my brother and sister. She made us do all of the cooking and housework and laundry. She hit us if we did not do our work quickly enough. I was afraid of her. I became sensitive and did not trust women any longer. I grew bitter. I looked to my father for help, but he did not understand. He was too busy with the farm and trying to forget our mother. He did not hear my cry for help. So, I stopped crying. I stopped going to school because I had too much work. I helped to take care of Thomas and Sophia so that they would not be hit and yelled at. I tried to save them from the pain that I felt. I kept hoping that someday my mother would return and that we would all be okay again, but she did not. She did not return. So I worked and I waited for better days.

Coming to America

In 1921, Chrisoula and her brother came to America. They

sailed to the west on a Greek ship, the King Alexander. She spent a year working as an embroiderer in New York City. After meeting my grandfather on two occasions in 1922, and less than a month after the first meeting, Chrisoula married George Caldes at the tender age of twenty-two.

For many years, things went well for Chrisoula and George as they welcomed three children into their lives, two daughters and then a son. George's restaurant prospered and he served the Governor of New York many times each week. Chrisoula and George had the home of their dreams, high-end cars, and everything material that their hearts desired. In addition, they had three healthy children and each other. They were happy.

It must have been very hard for George to lose his business, but he was of generous heart and kept all of his employees working until the bitter end. He and his restaurant went down in 1932 as a result of The Great Depression. He could not bear to tell his wife, so he kept the loss of the business a secret for a brief period of time. Shortly thereafter, Chrisoula took a walk and found her husband's restaurant boarded up and closed down. It was at that time that her problems began to emerge.

Chrisoula developed extreme anxiety in response to her husband's business collapse and began to develop troubling symptoms, alternating between being very sad and being out of control. She withdrew to her room, prayed and talked to herself. She was very excitable during this period. After a month of her illness, my grandfather sent her to visit friends where she showed marked improvement almost immediately. Soon, she returned home with no further symptoms for over two years.

In 1935, an agent of the gas company showed up at Chrisoula's home to turn off the meter since the gas bill had not been paid. This evidence of financial difficulty sent Chrisoula into a downward spiral with major symptoms of anxiety rising once again. My grandfather immediately sent her to visit with her brother in New York, and once again, she recovered quickly and was able to return home to her husband and children.

For unknown reasons, although I am sure that they must have been associated with security, Chrisoula suffered a third attack before Christmas of 1936 and a fourth attack at Easter of 1937, both important holiday seasons that required extra finances. However, on both of these occasions, Chrisoula recovered quickly.

Chrisoula became ill again just before Christmas of 1937, once again upset about lack of finances to support the holiday season. She retreated to her room, refused to have Christmas dinner and knocked down the Christmas tree. Shortly thereafter, my grandfather found her exhibiting violence toward their youngest child, my father, and brought her to the hospital for an evaluation. She was subsequently transferred to the Hudson River State Hospital in February of 1938 for observation and treatment.

It must have been very difficult for my grandfather to bring her to the hospital. In the past, he had always kept her home and given her the feeling of safety so that she could recover. He knew of her sensitivities and wanted her to know that she would not be left or abandoned. But he could do this no longer for she had become a danger not only to herself, but also to her children. The record shows that Chrisoula could not acknowledge the violence she acted out on her own child and spoke of the incident as if she had harmed herself. What pain this must have caused for her. And, how would she emerge from the hospital with this terrible shame that she carried about what she had done to her son? Maybe she would not.

Chrisoula Speaks:

I was so lost in this terrible feeling that would come over me. It felt like I did not want to live. Yet, I did not want to die either. I could not see a bright future. My son, Teddy, was close to the age that I was when my mother died. I could not look at him when I was frightened without seeing my younger self, the destroyed younger self that wept for years after her mother died. In these moments, Teddy was a manifestation of me, something that I could not bear to live again. I hurt him in a moment of rage at what was done to me. I took out decades of pain on him. I violated his trust as mine had been violated. My psyche tried to settle the score with my mother for leaving me, with my stepmother for abusing me and with my father for abandoning me emotionally. But, I settled nothing. I only furthered the destruction in an attempt to stifle all that tortured me. I want my children to know that I am so sorry.

Leaving Home

And so Chrisoula's journey in the Hudson River State Hospital began. Her first visit began in February of 1938, but she emerged on parole about a month later. They said that she was pleasant and helpful and enjoyed the various activities available for her entertainment. She spoke of her handwork. She liked to make things for her house. She wanted to go home and care for her children.

She went home for two months, only to return to the hospital after being upset by a man on a stretcher at the hospital where she received outpatient care twice per month. No one knows what the man said or why it upset her, but I can only imagine that it hit a deep nerve for her because it sent her straight back to the asylum! What happened?

Chrisoula Speaks:

He frightened me that day. I had been home for two months and was doing well with my husband and children and housework. I really was okay. But, he was a crazy man and he told me that I was going to die because I was evil. He scared me. I was afraid that he was right, for I had done bad things when I became sick. I didn't want to be sick again, but trying to get better was getting harder and harder with each attack. With each attack, I lost faith in myself. I knew that I couldn't endure the pain of losing my mother again. Being left in the hospital felt just like losing my mother. I was alone and afraid. Some people were cruel to me. I started to fall apart again that night, and this time, it would be for a long time. Teddy started to refer to himself as "The Golden Greek." This was his way of keeping me with him.

A Disturbing Departure

Chrisoula entered a downward spiral after her last entry to the hospital. She endured fourteen years of misunderstanding, loneliness and barbaric medical treatment before succumbing to death after undergoing a frontal lobotomy. The loss of her life was an unspeakable tragedy. What is left unfinished?

Chrisoula Speaks:

I left this world without the opportunity to say all that needed to be said. My only desire now is to shine my light upon my descendants. I am so proud of all of you! Your understanding of my life and death has brought me peace. The cycles of pain and addiction are done. Now, I rest.

Chapter 25
Birthing Our Dreams
By Kellie Meisl

You need chaos in your soul to give birth to a dancing star.
— Friedrich Nietzsche

I observe a large, dark gray, plump-looking airplane with a long red chute that curves upward on the sides. The chute extends from the plane's door to the ground. I am to enter this plane with a group of women, one my friend Connie. I am afraid to climb the chute. There is a ladder beside it, but it is rickety. A young, athletic woman climbs the chute and makes it up before me. On the ground, a male stands assisting women as they climb. He offers to help me ascend. I make the climb, then turn to observe the chute from above and notice that a section, in the middle, has become detached. I watch in fear as two young women hang from the detached part of the chute by their knees, upside down, to fix the section. However, they are carefree and relaxed.

I am now in the very spacious plane; many women are with me. I realize we were all supposed to bring our babies aboard, but no one did. I see a stack of empty cradles. My eyes become fixed upon an older woman who is walking around continuously. Her hair is fluffy, grayish white, and she wears pajamas, a robe and slippers. I realize we were all supposed to be wearing our pajamas but only the older woman is doing so. Yet, I get the sense that not wearing pajamas is right, what has been agreed upon.

On the same night Connie dreams she is one of many women on a maternity ward, wearing a robe and slippers. She is shuffling around the maternity ward; she has just given birth to her son. I am there with her.

There are many aspects of this dream that still elude me, though I dreamed it a decade ago and have pondered it ever since. I am not certain why the women in my dream agree upon not wearing pajamas or why this is the "right" choice. And where are the babies? Why is there a bunch of empty cradles? I do know two things. One, the dream was a shared dream. Connie and I both shared a dreamscape that night, a maternity ward full of women, some wearing robes and slippers. And two, my dream was a reflection of giving birth. The blimp-like plane with the long red chute is a symbol for the birthing process. I believe the fact that the chute became detached and that the women hang upon it, suspended, reflects my placental abruption and subsequent cesarean section. Perhaps the empty cradles are signs of the babies being whisked away from their mothers after surgery, as was mine.

Recently, I have come to understand that dreams of giving birth are life metaphors. They signal us, reminding us to birth our dreams, to create and bring forth the labor of our creation. The dreams will continue to recur until we take notice. And what if we do not heed the message of our birth dreams? Then the message is presented in the circumstances we face in the waking world where again we have the opportunity to take notice and create the dream we have been incubating.

Because I had given birth to my son not long before my birthing dream, I understood the dream first on a more literal level. Of course that was one layer of meaning to my dream. Then I had another more potent dream that caused me to take notice and look at things from a different angle.

Hospital Bed

I am lying in a hospital bed hooked up to many tubes, as I was after my cesarean section. I feel weak, like I am fading away. My doctor comes into the room. He is kind and gentle.

He shares with me that I have something growing in my abdomen. I fear it is uterine cancer. I know it is serious and that it will require great effort to recover, but I have hope that I can heal.

I awoke from this dream quite shaken and concerned. I knew it was important, and I knew on some level the growth in my abdomen signified something that *was* growing inside of me and needed to come out. At the time of the dream, I was just beginning to dabble in creating art. I understood that the uterus is located in the second chakra, the area of one's creativity. I saw the dream as a reminder to create and I continued with my art. I have created pieces for annual art shows held locally every year since, as well as pieces for family, friends and myself. I knew too the book I had wanted to write needed to manifest, and I began writing stories. Now that book, a labor of love, will be published soon. I also brought to fruition a book for children that I wrote and illustrated for my son. This is a project I dreamed of doing as an elementary teacher when I read and observed meaningfully written and beautifully illustrated works by others. And, I continue to work with dreams both formally in the classes I teach and privately as I work with my own dreams. I have never forgotten my *Hospital Bed* dream, and I realize how important it is for me to create on a regular basis.

Not long ago, I heard a story of a woman I knew as an acquaintance who died from cancer. Her cancer had originally grown in her abdomen but had healed. Then it returned in her uterus. The story I heard was astonishing. It led me to wonder if perhaps she did not have the chance to live the dream she held for herself.

The story came from her employer, a friend of mine. We were having tea, talking about dreams and she told me this story:

Prior to her death, Angela had been appointed to a new position within the company she was working for. This was one of several new assignments she had received in a period of a few short years. She liked this latest job and was now ready to stay with this new role for a while. She was finally feeling comfortable. Not too long after Angela settled in to her job, a woman she worked closely with, who was slated to move to another position within the company, had a miscarriage. The woman, Susan, had not been keen on changing her position in the first place. One day, Angela sat in the office of her boss in tears, a meeting she had called to say, "I cannot allow Susan to be involuntarily moved to this new position after the devastation she has suffered. Though I do not want to, I will take the new job." Very soon after, Angela became ill with uterine cancer. She wound up leaving her job shortly after taking it and never returned before her death.

This story stands as a powerful reminder to me that we cannot sell ourselves out; we must take care to create and follow the path that feels right to us, even if we feel pressure from others around us. Perhaps the older woman with white hair in my birthing dream stood out because she was enlightened; she chose to wear her pajamas and slippers though the younger women agreed it was right to conform.

As I peruse back through my dream journal, I note many metaphors of birth, some more direct than others. I notice I often dream of eggs, Easter eggs, cartons of eggs and jeweled eggs.

Gift of Eggs

I bump into a teacher who in waking life is deceased. I am surprised to see her. She tells me I must come to her home so she can give me something. Later, I learn my husband is going right by her home and I ask him to pick up the package. He tells me he cannot. I am confused as her house is not far from where he is going. I leave to go to her home myself. When I get there I realize she is no longer there but she has left me a package, a half dozen eggs with a note telling me they are for the children.

In another dream about eggs, I cannot find the eggs, though I know they are somewhere:

Lost Eggs

I am at the home of my in laws. I am helping my sister-in-law place Easter eggs for a big Easter egg hunt. I go to retrieve a bag of eggs I decorated specifically for the hunt but cannot find them. My sister-in-law becomes frustrated with me. I search and search and finally locate them in the closet.

In still another dream of eggs, I am shopping with a friend, who is a teacher and I discover many eggs in an unexpected place:

Bejeweled Eggs

I am shopping with Cathy. I am in a teaching supplies store looking for items for my classroom. I do not see any traditional classroom items. Instead, I come across shelves of jeweled eggs in every color. I decide to purchase some of these beautiful items and forego the traditional classroom implements.

I feel fortunate that I have these dreams documented. I remind myself it is important to reread them now and then. When I read the dreams, I can see that as I was having them, they were little seeds growing into the life I now have. Many aspects of the dreams have played out. I realize now that the dreaming mind is a vessel where the offspring of our soul's aspirations may nest. All we need to do is allow ourselves to slumber, then remember and honor our dreams; that alone will help us fulfill a more conscious role in how our lives unfold. So I will do my personal best to bring my dreams into existence. And, if I can do anything to honor Angela's dream, it will be to remember to exercise extreme self-care when making important decisions about my life's path. I will take on the roles I love and create what is meaningful to me, even if I feel pressured to do otherwise. My life's purpose has its own design and I must be willing to descry it; this is how I will birth my dreams.

Concluding *Wisdom*
Your Inner Mystic is Your Healer and Guide
By Connie Caldes and Kellie Meisl

What is a friend? A single soul dwelling in two bodies.
— Aristotle

We felt compelled to tell our stories because the sharing that has ensured in our friendship has been deeply healing for both of us. We have explored our inner worlds together. We have been mirrors for each other. We have no secrets. We truly know each other on an intimate level.

We encourage you to explore your inner world with others and to experience the magic in those relationships. There is nothing more healing than being known and loved. The following may help you in your explorations:

What We Have Learned About Dreams:

Dreams act as signposts, guiding us on our journey through life.

Dreams bring that which is unconscious into consciousness. Even the smallest fragment may have great meaning.

Dreams are springboards from which our creative forces emerge.

Dreams introduce us to many layers of our physical, emotional, mental and spiritual selves by presenting us with a cast of characters, all of whom reside somewhere within us.

Dreams introduce us to our hidden desires.

Dreams teach us of the condition of humanity as a whole.

Dreams, waking life, mediation and shamanic journeys are all part of a continuum. They contain metaphors that *speak* to us by bringing our attention to issues, things that we need to look at, and by giving us guidance on how to navigate and heal those issues.

Dreams of the shadow self are often presented in dark imagery. These dreams bring us in touch with the parts of ourselves that we have banished and provide an opportunity to embrace our lost essence, which can pivot our life into the opposite direction of the shadow, into the light.

Dreams give us the opportunity to consciously choose the archetypes and metaphors that we live by. With this conscious choice, our lives move toward healing and purpose rather than the dysfunction of unconscious enactment.

Dreams make us healed and whole; they reacquaint us with our heart and soul.

We could not be born had we not first grown in a place of darkness and then, moving through it, emerged from the spiritual waters into the place of light.

Epilogue
Dream Stories Heal
By Connie Caldes

Upon completion of this manuscript, I struggled with telling the story of my grandmother and how my family might feel about it. I wrote to my cousin, George Glassanos, my Aunt Connie's oldest son, and the oldest grandson of Chrisoula and George Caldes. I shared *Chrisoula's Story* with him and received the gift of the following words from him:

Connie:

I do not think your father could ever be offended by what you've written; it is an amazing chronicle. It will certainly tap right into the part of him that makes him feel as he does. And, it will probably suggest to him that he is so loved by his Mom that he might try to let go of the other feelings. It is never too late if you are living. Not to try, or not to have a chance to try... that would be... When I read your work, I accept it as the truth. It is true for me and I'm real happy you've done this. Why? It jives with what I think happened, how our grandmother felt, how she thought of herself and her little boy. How she wished things had worked out differently, for everyone. When you look at Connie and Helen and Ted, how they've managed to do all they did thru their own lives, how can you come to any conclusion other than she must have been a remarkable lady. Papou was an exceptional person... we know that because we all knew him. But we did not know Chrisoula... at least I didn't know her, and as a consequence, I always attributed all the positive, familial traits to Papou. Well, that was clearly incorrect.

I try to call my Mom every Friday night as I make my way down the Pike to the Cape to be with Lee who I've adored since I was 17. Last Friday night, my mother and I were talking about her Mom and Dad a little and my mother mentioned she thought Papou was still watching over us. I mentioned that you are writing and that from your writing I got the notion that her Mom was watching over us as well, with Papou... not separated from each other any more. She agreed. And then she told me this and I had to bite my lip to keep tears away. She said, "I want to see her again."

I think what you are doing is enormous. It is to me! Do what your instincts tell you to do without hesitation... I love you, too... Geor

Bibliography

Books

Andrews, Ted, *Animal Speak*. St. Paul: Llewellyn Publications, 1993.

Bach, Richard, *Illusions: The Adventures of a Reluctant Messiah*, London: Arrow Books, Ltd., 2001.

Bach, Richard, *One*. New York: Dell, 1989.

Bach, Richard, *The Bridge Across Forever, A Love Story*. New York: William Morrow & Co., 1984.

Barasch, Marc Ian, *Healing Dreams*, New York: Riverhead Books, 2000.

Berman, Bob, and Robert Lanza, *Biocentrism: How Life and Consciousness Are the Keys to Understanding the True Nature of the Universe*. Dallas: Benbella Books, 2000.

Berman, Bob, *Cosmic Adventure: Other Secrets Beyond the Night Sky*. New York: Harper Perennial, 2000.

Berman, Bob, *Secret of the Night Sky*. New York: Harper Paperbacks, 1996.

Bolen, Jean Shinoda, *Close to the Bone: Life Threatening Illness and the Search for Meaning*. New York, Scribner, 1998.

Bolen, Jean Shinoda, *Goddesses in Everywoman: A New Psychology of Women*. New York: Harper Perennial, 1985.

Chodorow, Nancy, *The Power of Feelings, Personal Meaning in Psychoananlysis, Gender, and Culture*. New Haven: Yale University Press, 1999.

Dale, Cyndi, *New Chakra Healing: The Revolutionary 32-Center Energy System*, St. Paul: Llewelln Publications, 1997.

Eliade, Mircea, *Shamanism: Archaic Techniques of Ecstasy*. Princeton: Princeton University Press, 1964.

Garfield, Patricia, *Creative Dreaming*. New York: Fireside, 1974.

Grabhorn, Lynn, *Excuse Me, Your Life is Waiting: The Astonishing Power of Feelings*. Charlottesville: Hampton Roads Publishing Company, Inc., 2003.

Harner, Michael, *The Way of the Shaman*. New York: HarperCollins, 1990.

Hicks, Esther and Jerry, *The Law of Attraction: The Basics of the Teachings of Abraham*. Carlsbad: Hay House, 2006.

Ingerman, Sandra, *Medicine for the Earth*. New York: Three Rivers Press, 2000.

Ingerman, Sandra, *Soul Retrieval: Mending the Fragmented Self*. New York: HarperCollins, 1991.

Kharitidi, Olga, *Entering the Circle: Ancient Secrets of Siberian Wisdom Discovered by a Russian Psychiatrist*. New York: HarperOne, 1997.

Kharitidi, Olga, *The Master of Lucid Dreams*. Charlottesville: Hampton Roads Publishing Company, Inc., 2001.

Krippner, Stanley, *The Mythic Path*. New York: G.P. Putnam's Sons, 1997.

Norwood, Robin, *Women Who Love Too Much*. New York: Pocket, 2008

Pinkola Estes, Clarissa, *Women Who Run With the Wolves*. New York: Ballantine Books, 1992.

Porter, Margit Esser, *Hope Lives: The After Breast Cancer Treatment Survival Handbook*. Peterborough: h.i.c. publishing, 2000.

Ringgold, Faith, *Tar Beach*. Albuquerque: Dragonfly Books, 1996.

Sams, Jamie, *Medicine Cards*. New York: St. Martin's Press, 1988.

Sedgwick, Catharine, *Personal Papers*. Massachusetts Historical Society, Boston, MA.

Siegel, Bernie, *Love, Medicine and Miracles*. New York: Harper Paperbacks, 1990.

Some, Malidoma, *The Healing Wisdom of Africa*. New York: Penguin Putnam Inc., 1998.

Taylor, Jeremy, *The Living Labyrinth: Exploring Universal Themes in Myths, Dreams, and the Symbolism of Waking Life*. Mahwah: Paulist Press, 1998.

Walsch, Neil Donald, *Conversations with God, an uncommon dialogue*. New York: Putnam Adult, 1996.

Wilds, Mary, Mumbet: *The Life and Times of Elizabeth Freeman*. Greensboro: Avisson Press Inc., 1999.

Audio/Music

Cecilia, *Voice of the Femine Spirit* [CD]. 1999.

Myss, Caroline, *Energy Anatomy: The Science of Personal Power, Spirituality, and Health* [CD]. Louisville: Sounds True, Inc., 2001.

Naparstek, Belleruth, *Health Journeys: A Meditation to Help You With Radiation Therapy* [CD]. Akron: Health Journeys, 1999.

Rondstadt, Linda, *Linda Rondstadt: Greatest Hits* [CD]. 1976.

Video

Field of Dreams, Phil Alden Robinson. Gordon Company, 1989.

Last of the Mohicans. Michael Mann. Morgan Creek Productions, 1992.

Recommended Reading

Dream Network Journal

A New Earth by Eckhart Tolle

Anatomy of the Spirit by Caroline Myss

Animal Speak by Ted Andrews

Animal Wise by Ted Andrews

Astral Dynamics by Robert Bruce

Close to the Bone by Jean Shinoda Bolen

Conversations With God by Neale Donald Walsh

Creative Dreaming by Patricia Garfield

Dreamgates by Robert Moss

Dreaming While Awake by Arnold Mindell

Dreams are Letters from the Soul by Connie Kaplan

Eastern Body, Western Mind by Anodea Judith

Energy Medicine by Donna Eden

Entering the Circle by Olga Kharitidi, MD

Excuse Me, Your Life is Waiting by Lynn Grabhorn

Far Journeys by Robert Monroe

From Science to God by Peter Russell

Goddesses in Every Woman by Jean Shinoda Bolen

Hands of Light by Barbara Brennan

Healing Dreams by Marc Ian Barasch

Healing Toxic Thoughts by Sandra Ingerman

Illusions by Richard Bach

Imagery in Healing by Jeanne Achterberg

In the Shadow of the Shaman by Amber Wolfe

Journeys Out of the Body by Robert Monroe

Love is in the Earth by Melody

Medicine Cards by Jamie Sams and David Carson

Medicine for the Earth by Sandra Ingerman

New Chakra Healing by Cyndi Dale

Of Water and the Spirit by Malidoma Patrice Some

One by Richard Bach

Our Dreaming Mind by Robert Van deCastle

Owning Your Own Shadow by Robert A. Johnson

Sacred Contracts by Caroline Myss

Shaman, Healer, Sage by Alberto Villoldo

Shamanic Journeying: A Beginner's Guide by Sandra Ingerman

Soul Retrieval by Sandra Ingerman

Staying Well With Guided Imagery by Belleruth Naparstek

The Active Side of Infinity by Carlos Castenada

The Art of Dreaming by Carlos Castaneda

The Artist's Way by Julia Cameron

The Bridge Across Forever by Richard Bach

The Celestine Prophecy by James Redfield

The Dance by Oriah Mountain Dreamer

The Four Agreements by Don Miguel Ruiz

The Healing Wisdom of Africa by Malidoma Some

The Kin of Ata are Waiting for you by Dorothy Bryant

The Last Hours of Ancient Sunlight by Thom Hartman

The Living Labyrinth by Jeremy Taylor

The Mists of Avalon by Marion Zimmer Bradley

The Mythic Path by Stanley Krippner

The Power of Myth by Joseph Campbell

Dream Stories

The Subtle Body by Cyndi Dale

The Woman's Book of Dreams by Connie Kaplan

The Woman's Dictionary of Symbols and Objects by Barbara Walker

The Woman's Encyclopedia of Myths and Secrets by Barbara Walker

Tracking Freedom by Ken Eagle Feather

Ultimate Journey by Robert Monroe

Vibrational Medicine for the 21st Century by Richard Gerber

Waking the Global Heart by Anodea Judith

Waking the Tiger: Healing Trauma by Peter Levine

Way of the Shaman by Michael Harner

Welcome Home by Sandra Ingerman

Where People Fly and Water Runs Uphill by Jeremy Taylor

Women Who Run With the Wolves by Clarissa Pinkola Estes

Women's Bodies, Women's Wisdom by Christiane Northrup

Recommended Audio

A New Earth by Eckhart Tolle

Anam Cara by John O'Donahue

Dream Interpretation by Clarissa Pinkola Estes

Energy Anatomy by Caroline Myss

Making the Gods Work For You by Caroline Casey

Sitting by the Well by Marion Woodman

The Artist's Way by Julia Cameron

The Soul Retrieval Journey by Sandra Ingerman

The Theater of Imagination by Clarrisa Pinkola Estes

LaVergne, TN USA
26 August 2009

155942LV00002B/1/P